Earth's crammed with heaven,
And every common bush afire with God;
But only he who sees, takes off his shoes –
The rest sit round it and pluck blackberries.

Elizabeth Barrett Browning, *Aurora Leigh*, IIV

🌿 THE NATIONAL TRUST

Sacred Places

Spirit and Landscape

Crispin Paine

To my mother
remembering a pilgrimage

First published in 2004 by
National Trust Enterprises Ltd
36 Queen Anne's Gate, London SW1H 9AS

www.nationaltrust.org.uk

Cataloguing in Publication Data is available from the British Library

ISBN 0 7078 03721

Design by Barbara Mercer
Map by Oxford Designers & Illustrators
Origination by Digital Imaging Ltd, Glasgow
Printed and bound in Singapore by Star Standard Printing Ltd, c/o Weygraphic Limited

front cover (clockwise from top left): Maori Hut, Clandon Park; Glastonbury Tor; Sutton Hoo, Suffolk; Uffington White Horse; Avebury Stone Circle; Giant's Causeway; Fountains Abbey cellarium.

back cover (from top): Castlerigg Circle; St Michael's Mount.

page 1: Burial mound at Sutton Hoo.

page 2: Seascape at the Farne Islands, Northumberland.

CONTENTS

INTRODUCTION

Throughout the ages people have called particular places 'sacred', 'holy' or taboo. These places have been as small as a single stone and as great as a country or landscape, but all have been imbued with a special quality and have been treated differently from ordinary places. That understanding of what is meant by 'special' has varied greatly from age to age and culture to culture, but the way in which people have behaved towards the sacred place has shown remarkable consistency. For anthropologists who study them in depth, ceremonies of dedication share distinct similarities; pilgrimage differs remarkably little in practice, even where pilgrims give very varying explanations of what they are doing; specific sites such as caves, mountains and springs have been selected for veneration in widely differing cultures and ages.

A couple of generations ago, for most people the term 'sacred place' would have meant churches and monasteries. Today, though many point to a decline in the influence of established religion in everyday life, interest in the spiritual in a wider sense appears to be growing. Every music festival has its 'spirit zone', and there is widespread interest in holy wells, stone circles, and places credited with a 'spiritual' atmosphere. Moreover, easier travel has made people familiar with the sacred places of many other countries, traditions and religions.

England, Wales and Northern Ireland have their fair share of places which are today, or have been in the past, seen as in some sense 'sacred'. The aim of this book is to signal and to celebrate sacred places that are cared for by the National Trust, and this introduction sets out to put them into a worldwide context, and to suggest a number of answers to the question 'what is a sacred place'?

The National Trust has acquired a portfolio of such places, ranging from strange and myth-imbued landscape features, such as the Giant's Causeway on the Antrim Coast (see p.50); through places which in the past were seen as sacred, such as the great stone circle at Avebury, Wiltshire (see p.28); to places like Glastonbury Tor in Somerset, which modern New-Age devotees now visit in very large numbers (see p.52), much as Glastonbury Abbey attracted huge numbers of Christian pilgrims in medieval times. This book examines a selection of these places, and from them seeks to develop an understanding of the sacred place in some of the traditions of the UK and the wider world.

The National Trust has acquired its sacred sites almost by chance – most were bought or given either because they were part of a beautiful landscape, or because of their historic and artistic interest. And of course,

opposite: Castlerigg Circle, Cumbria.

some traditions are very much better represented than others – there are many more medieval monasteries and prehistoric ceremonial sites, for example, than sites which reflect some of the newer spiritual traditions, or those traditions comparatively new to the British Isles. Even so, it is remarkable what a very large number of such places there are in the Trust's care. In terms of buildings, churches, chapels, and monasteries are the obvious examples to include. But there are also natural features revered as holy, such as mountains (*see* The Holy Mountain, p.84), rivers and streams (*see* Nature Worship, p.40), wells (*see* Holy Wells, p.58), caves (*see* Mithras and the Cave, p.60) and islands. Places that have acquired a holiness through association include the dwellings of Dark Age saints (*see* Nature and Celtic Spirituality, p.46) and the sites of Victorian Revivalist 'camp meetings' (*see* Revivalism and Camp Meetings, p.74). Moreover, whole landscapes can become 'sacred places' when people attribute to them powers of spiritual renewal (*see* The Spiritual Landscape, p.64).

There are parallels, too, to be drawn between the origins and work of the National Trust and the very notion of the sacred place. When the Trust was founded at the end of the nineteenth century, its genesis lay in the social reform movements of that time – principally the need to liberate workers imprisoned in industrial cities by providing free access to land on which they could walk, dream and find their spirits refreshed. This belief in the regenerative power of landscape has always underlain the Trust's work. Octavia Hill, one of the original founders, described nature and the outdoors thus: 'It belongs to you all, to every landless man, woman and child in England'. For her, it was nothing less than 'God's passionate inheritance', and this feeling was reflected in the words of a Sheffield factory-worker who donated 2s 2d to the organisation with the words: 'All my life I have longed to see the Lakes. I shall never see them now, but I should like to keep them there for others.'

The historian G.M. Trevelyan, writing of the Trust in wartime, wrote:

> But the need to preserve natural beauty, both by the National Trust and otherwise, is not merely a question of preserving holiday grounds for masses of people from the town. It is also a matter of preserving a main source of spiritual wellbeing and inspiration, on which our ancestors throve and which we are in danger of losing forever. Unless we can refresh ourselves at least by intermittent contact with nature, we grow awry... Like the universe, like life, natural beauty also is a mystery. But whatever it may be,

BRANDELHOW
THE FIRST PROPERTY OF THE
NATIONAL TRUST IN THIS DISTRICT
WAS OPENED ON 16TH OCTOBER 1902 BY
H. R. H. THE PRINCESS LOUISE
FOUR OAKS WERE PLANTED HERE BY
PRINCESS LOUISE
MISS OCTAVIA HILL
SIR ROBERT HUNTER
CANON H. D. RAWNSLEY.

... natural beauty is the ultimate spiritual appeal of the universe, of nature, or of the God of nature, to their nursling man. It and it alone makes a common appeal to the sectaries of all our religious and scientific creeds, to the lovers of all our different schools of poetry and art, ancient and modern, and to many more beside these. It is the highest common denominator in the spiritual life of today.

Commemorative plaque at Brandelhow Park, Derwentwater, marking the site of the first National Trust property in the Lake District, 1902.

above: Fountains Abbey,
North Yorkshire.

below: The cellarium at
Fountains Abbey.

What is a 'Sacred Place'?

The key characteristic of the sacred place is perhaps the most obvious one: that it is distinct from everywhere else. The sacred place is set apart, and guarded by physical, ritual and psychological barriers (*see* Sanctuary, p.92). People approaching the sacred place are often expected to show their realisation that this place is very special by some form of ritual, which may include washing, removing footwear, donning or removing headgear, genuflection, or making an offering of money or flowers. Moreover, there are frequently gradations of sacredness within the space or building: the ark is the most sacred part of a synagogue, the sanctuary that of a church, while a Hindu temple, like the ancient Jewish temple, has a subtle gradation of sacred spaces, the most holy of which are accessible only by priests in a state of ritual purity.

It is, of course, important to remember the thread that runs through most religions that denies entirely the possibility of any space being specifically sacred (*see* Questioning the Sacred Place, p.70). If God is everywhere, how can He be anywhere in particular? St Augustine said: 'God is everywhere, it is true, and He that made all things is not confined to dwell in one place'.

Taking this view, making a pilgrimage to a specific place is useless:

> My sacred shrine of pilgrimage is spiritual wisdom within ... The spiritual wisdom given by the Guru is the True sacred shrine of pilgrimage... (Guru Nanak, founder of Sikhism);
> When the Lord invites the blest to their inheritance in the kingdom of Heaven, He does not include a pilgrimage to Jerusalem amongst their good deeds (Gregory of Nyssa).

Another view sees sacred places as sites where the divine is particularly concentrated. This is the view the Catholic tradition takes of churches (*see* Restoring the Altar, p.94), and was the view of the third-century pagan philosopher, Plotinus:

> I think, therefore, that those ancient sages, who sought to secure the presence of divine beings by the erection of shrines and statues, showed insight into the nature of the All; they perceived that, though this Soul is everywhere tractable, its presence will be secured all the more readily when an appropriate receptacle is elaborated, a place especially capable of receiving some portion or phase of it, something reproducing it, or representing it, and serving like a mirror to catch an image of it.

The North Cloister Walk at Lacock Abbey, Wiltshire.

The great Romanian scholar of religion, Mircea Eliade (1907–1986), saw the sacred place as a spot where the membrane dividing the realm of the gods, of grace and of the transcendent, from the world of humanity, of nature, and of the immanent, becomes thin. The barrier between Heaven and Earth can be crossed. The sacred place has also been seen as a 'focusing lens' that concentrates attention on the activities going on within it, and thus reveals their true religious meaning. Other students of religion, interpreting the term more liberally, have attempted to classify the different 'sacred' kinds of special place.

A more liberal view still would include within the definition a wide spectrum of places that are special. One can identify six types of sacred place: places to which spiritual meaning is attributed; places of memory; places of immanent energy; places created specifically to convey spiritual feelings; places formally set apart by an institution; and places made holy by the presence of a holy object.

Places Credited with Spiritual Meaning

Our society has agreed to regard some landscapes both as beautiful, and (not quite so unanimously) as possessing a spiritual quality which can offer refreshment if approached in the right way. The Lake District was once merely a wild area of poor farming and worse communications, but it came to be seen by the Romantics as a landscape of grandeur, romance and spiritual renewal, and still today walking and thinking is regarded by some as the 'right' way to approach it, while speed-boating and paragliding is not.

In this very broad sense, every National Trust site is a special place, and the siting of the familiar oak-leaf marker is an act of dedication: a declaration that our society (or at least an important part of it) recognises this spot as different, in some sense that can be seen as spiritual.

Why do we regard some landscapes as 'beautiful'? There is nothing innate about seeing desert or sea or mountain as 'beautiful'; beauty lies entirely in the eye of the beholder. One learns to see particular kinds of scenery as beautiful, just as the adolescent learns to like the taste of beer or the generation of the 1920s learned to find the paintings of Picasso beautiful. All taste is culturally determined. In the West, the appreciation of landscape was closely associated with the Romantic Movement: a deliberate attempt by one particular generation of the ruling élite to favour emotion over reason. However, a taste for landscape is by no means confined to the West; it is one shared with, for example, the ruling élite of China and Japan over many generations.

Is to appreciate a landscape, or feel a sentimental attachment to a particular place, the same thing as regarding it as 'sacred'? At first glance, perhaps, they seem very different experiences based on even more different explanations. Yet we speak of the 'spiritual power' – the potential for renewal – offered by wild and beautiful places, and while more people no doubt seek such refreshment by walking in the hills than by going on retreat, the motive is perhaps very similar. I suggest that they are all part of a continuum of attitude that sees particular sites as special, and that includes places imbued with memory; places imbued with special meaning; places seen as possessed of power; and places both sacred and forbidden.

Appreciation of landscape is usually understood as looking, and then developing a sentiment: emotion follows view follows expectation. This was how the Romantics understood it. It is also the process behind many a religious cult. The devotee looks at the image worshipfully, and his or her emotion is stirred. If they are lucky, they will discover an altered state of consciousness, and such an experience will confirm and develop their devotion. This is the experience of the Hindu devotee taking *darshan* of the temple image, of the Catholic before the Host (the bread consecrated in the Mass) at Benediction, and also, I suggest, of many a hill-walker looking out over Wastwater from Scafell Pike.

Of course, people have to learn this reaction, which is often indeed fostered very consciously. Convent children are taught what feelings they should be cultivating when adoring the Host; the traveller is taught (by innumerable guidebooks) what sentiments to foster when confronted with the famous view.

The cult of landscape is one of the strangest developments of Western culture. Why should one generation – of the most sophisticated and educated people – regard only the most manicured and obviously-cultivated countryside as beautiful, while another finds romance and the perfection of beauty in wild mountain scenery? It can be argued that every beauty is culturally determined and that nobody finds anything beautiful without having been taught to do so. Of course, there are pioneers. Admirers of Victorian industrial buildings were as scarce in the 1930s as admirers of mountains in the 1680s (and famously, the young Mozart did not once glance out at the – to our eyes – awe-inspiring view when journeying across the Alps), but over a generation these pioneers taught others to share their quirky enthusiasm.

We can only make guesses at the reasons that lead to new understandings of beauty. Appreciation of the 'picturesque' in the West was closely linked to the Romantic movement in philosophy and the arts, and can be seen as a product of the rising entrepreneurial class, looking for an escape from the mines and factories that were the real source of their wealth.

'Picturesque' originally meant suitable for a picture, and it was the view that dominated the way in which landscape was experienced. Is viewing the only way in which people experience the 'sacred place'?

Surely not: the pilgrim who approaches the shrine on his or her knees, who rings the temple bell, feeds the sacred fish, eats the blessed bread, drinks the holy water, rubs the foot of St Peter's statue in Rome, is experiencing the sacred place with all four senses. Sometimes the experience is drastic: the rites commonly held at some sacred places can be both painful and terrifying.

But the beautiful landscape is not the only kind credited with spiritual power or meaning. For the early Christian hermits, the desert was not beautiful: it was a place of fear and threat. Its value lay precisely in its emptiness, where the Christian could struggle with the inner and outer demons without distraction. The desert – and later the western 'deserts', the islands of western Europe – was originally seen as holy not just because it was full of holy men, but because it offered a blank canvas on which the holy man could write his spiritual life.

Places Made Sacred by Memory

The second group is by far the largest: places whose spiritual meaning has been written onto them by memory. Virtually everybody has somewhere that is special just to them. This may be the café where they first met their partner, or their favourite view, or they may share some special place with their close family. If so, they are agreeing to imbue that place with meaning in just the same way – albeit a less formal way – as a Church agrees to imbue a building with meaning by dedication, or a nation agrees to imbue a war memorial with meaning, or a society agrees to regard a particular landscape as beautiful.

The landscape is created by geological forces, by climate and by the farming, forestry, and the engineering and building activities of humankind. But it is memory that determines how we see and understand that landscape: the landscape that we know. Sometimes this landscape is created by personal memory: the associations of a familiar countryside with our holidays or our home. Sometimes it is created by a collective memory of folk experiences, of historical or traditional events. Sometimes it is created by myth – stories developed to explain and make useful the landscape as part of its people's underlying ideology. But always it is we who create this memory and hence this landscape. Different groups of people can see a very different landscape: the Scottish Highlands can be seen as a desert whose inhabitants have been wickedly expelled, or as a romantic holiday playground, or as an everyday working landscape.

So it is with sacred places. The places where significant events took place take on a 'specialness' that is the creation of collective memory. Battlefields are one secular example; the battlefields and cemeteries of the First World War are real places, but they have become places of very special meaning to the belligerent countries of Western Europe through the imposition on them of particular sets of memory and understanding (*see* A Place to Remember, p.86).

Such places made sacred by memory may be strictly historical, traditional, or purely mythical. Mow Cop in Cheshire is a place of special significance to Methodists because it was there that an historic gathering took place that led to the development of Primitive Methodism (*see* p.74). The Holy Sepulchre is a sacred place because Christians have traditionally seen it as the location where the great work of redemption of humankind happened. Dragon's Hill in Oxfordshire, immediately below the 3,000-year-old hillside chalk carving of a horse, is the location in myth of the battle between St George and the Dragon. In all three types of place memory has been imposed upon the land, and some of the power of the remembered event is still held to linger.

Sacred Landscape

For some, the term 'sacred place' implies a comparatively small area, but in fact many cultures have regarded the entire landscape, country or even continent as sacred, and many continue to do so today. Such a view is underpinned by the attachment of myths and legends to the landscape. Mountains, valleys, cities, rivers, lakes are given names and stories that contribute to a particular understanding of the land, and which associate it with its people.

The Gospels establish the notion of a Holy Land – a landscape presented to tell or support a story. And the history of Israel/Palestine is a story of competitive adaptation and remodelling by successive ideologies and regimes (*see* Holy Land and 'Crusade', p.78). The real landscape can appear quite different to people of different traditions, who notice different places within it, tell different stories about them, and call them by different names. Sometimes this competition is between a view of the land as sacred and another view of it as mundane. 'Holy Serbia' competes with a mere province of Yugoslavia; the Aborigines' view of Australia as a landscape of mystical significance and meaning (like the Native American's view of the traditional homelands in the US) competes with the secular one. To some, Wales is still 'Holy Wales', a sacred land and

Looking east-north-east from Carn Llidi up along the Pembroke coast to Strumble Head.

View from St David's
Head, Pembrokeshire.

a chosen people (*see* p.108). Sometimes one view of the land as sacred competes with an equivalent, quite contradictory view. India is a sacred landscape to the Hindu, but so it is to many Moslems: as the birthplace of Adam and the site of the first mosque.

Private Memory

For many people their home, or perhaps their childhood home, is the most special, most sacred place, of all. For some it is the only sacred place they acknowledge. The home is par excellence the place of memory; as Ruskin put it: 'This is the true nature of home – it is the place of peace, the shelter, not only from injury, but from all terror, doubt and division'. It is

tempting to assume that the association of 'home' with place is universal, but in fact for many the 'sacred' thing is not the home – house, furniture, memories – but rather the family. 'Home' may not be a particular house at all; Victorian farmworkers in southern England were accustomed to change their employer, and hence their place of residence, every year at the Candlemas hiring fair. The following conversation was overheard in the street in Dorchester in the late nineteenth century:

'Be you a-shifting this year, Lisa?'

'No, nor did I last year, but I was obliged to take the things all outside and turn 'em round a bit to make believe as how I'd shifted.'

right: View of the garden from the study window at Hardy's Cottage, Lower Brockhampton, Dorset.

below: Ancient Greek inscription over the doorway at T.E. Lawrence's cottage, Clouds Hill, Dorset, which translates as 'Why Worry?'

An equally powerful carrier of meaning may be a spot where a significant incident in a person's life took place, or which represents a focus of their ambition. But how they represent that meaning to themselves depends on their own belief and traditions. Thus Sibusiso Vilane, the first black African to climb Everest, recalled in 2003:

> As soon as I saw the flags, I started to think about my home and family. I fell to my knees and wept and prayed to the Lord to thank him for protecting me. After that, I got up and climbed to the flags. I felt it was a very sacred place, but I felt very welcome.

Private memory also creates sacred space at family graves. Even today the 'tidying-up' of a family grave – trimming of grass, renewing of flowers – is for many people a duty and a privilege. This simple act may indeed be the nearest many of us ever get to the kind of act of worship which in another culture we might perform at a shrine. In recent years this act of reverence and memory has been extended to the 'roadside shrine' to victims of traffic accidents; a public commemoration and a reproof. The scattering of ashes has become a way in which the individual can create a permanent link with a special place, in the most permanent way possible. The recent threat to redevelop York City Football club has revealed the number of individuals whose ashes have been spread there.

At the level of the community, too, the creation of sacred space is one of the principal ways in which we memorialise the dead. From the Taj Mahal to the Cenotaph, the creating of a space in which the dead are remembered enables those left behind to cope with their grief and loss (*see* The Tomb as Sacred Place, p.62). Such shrines are sometimes temporary, as for example the commemoration arranged every year for Armistice Day in the week around November 11th at Westminster Abbey, when individuals plant small poppy-crosses in the ground to remember the dead of two world wars and other conflicts, or the shrine-making that followed the Hillsborough Stadium disaster in 1989 and the death of Princess Diana in 1997. After the terrorist attacks on New York's twin towers on 11 September 2001, the photographs of lost loved ones which were pinned up at the site at Ground Zero was a visual marker and a confirmation that the place had become in some sense a shrine to the memory of those who died there.

Places Believed to Have Innate Sacredness or 'Energy'

So far we have considered varieties of sacred space where it is clear to all that the 'sacredness' has been attributed by people. There is, however, another kind where for some people the place itself is sacred, regardless of the beliefs, views and actions of human beings. The place would stay sacred even if no one believed it was. Such innate sacred character may be believed to be the action of a god, or it may be a phenomenon of nature, but it cannot be disputed or changed.

Places credited with such innate spiritual power are surprisingly common across many different cultures and ages. Holy mountains are found in many parts of the world, as are sacred caves and holy springs, wells and rivers. In India the junctions of rivers are considered to have particular power. Very often, this inherent spiritual power is thought to have been given to the place by a god or a holy person; recently, messengers from another planet have been credited with a similar power of blessing (the beliefs concerning the origins of crop circles, for example).

Many societies have seen nature as a force, exerting particular powers in particular places, which can be harnessed or benefited from by humankind, or which must be placated. In the West today that attitude is perhaps best evinced by the New Age belief in Ley Lines – channels of earth energy that run, almost like a National Grid, across the landscape and along which different sacred sites are found (St Michael's Mount in

Cornwall and Glastonbury Tor in Somerset are thought to be 'linked' in this way). The increasingly accepted Eastern idea of Feng Shui – the arrangement of landscape or home to ensure harmony and a beneficent environment – also reflects this way of thinking. This system concerns the distribution, by wind and water currents, of various terrestrial and atmospheric emanations that are believed to exert important influences on people. In China, and now also in the West, geomancers make a living by advising on the siting of homes within the landscape, and the design and arrangement of the home itself.

Places Created to Convey Spiritual Feelings

Another kind of sacred place we can identify is the place deliberately created in order to convey spiritual feelings. Of these, surely the garden is the most obvious.

> The kiss of the sun for pardon,
> The song of the birds for mirth,
> One is nearer God's Heart in a garden
> Than anywhere else on earth.

Dorothy Gurney's verse summarises an attitude to gardens that is by no means limited to early twentieth-century Protestant England. The word 'paradise' derives from the Old Persian word *pairidaeza*, meaning a garden or park, and for Christians, Jews and Moslems humankind originated in the Garden of Eden. The garden has been seen as a type of the heavenly abode in cultures ranging from ancient Japan (*see* Japanese Gardens, p.104) through medieval Islam to modern Britain. In many traditions gardens have been created as practical aids to devotion, places set aside to offer a taste of the eternal and an aid to the discovery of inner peace, truth and beauty.

Sacred Buildings

Even more common than gardens are buildings designed to generate in the visitor feelings of awe and reverence. In a palace it is the king whom one should venerate, but in a church or a temple it is God. Take away all those buildings designed to create such reverence and one has removed a great proportion of humankind's architectural heritage.

The architect of a sacred building needs to ensure that it fulfils three

right: The Japanese Garden at Greys Court, Oxfordshire.

below: The yew trees at Packwood House, Warwickshire.

below: Detail of *Acer palmatum* leaves from the Japanese Garden, Tatton Park, Cheshire.

criteria. It must symbolise the faith of which it is an expression; it must perform a practical function as a centre for rites and ceremonies; and it must inspire and uplift the visitor. The effort to 'bring visitors to their knees' is at the heart of what many architects are attempting in creating sacred buildings. This attempt is an extraordinarily complex business, involving an appeal to the familiar through the deployment of well-known forms; the use of surprise through new forms; the use of current vocabulary, or the vocabulary of a past time; and the use of form, texture and light in dramatic or soothing ways.

Besides aiming at the beautiful or the impressive, the designer has a choice of vocabulary, and in a building with religious connotations, this may well be a conscious revival of a past style. Many mosques in modern Britain make deliberate reference, in their domes and window-shapes, for example, to the style of the Mughul Empire. Only comparatively recently have the architects of churches abandoned reference to the Gothic style, the revival of which said so much to Victorian England (*see* Gothic Revival, p.80).

Detail of dove from stained glass window, Tyntesfield Chapel, Somerset.

No building can easily avoid carrying a weight of symbolism. In some this is very deliberate. The siting, layout and design of the Hindu temple are governed by scriptures; every stone is intended to set forth the temple's role as the meeting place between gods and people. The Christian church often has the plan of a cross, and mystical writers have seen symbolism in every window and wall, column and spire. In other buildings the symbolism is there, but at a much deeper level, perhaps only at the level where architecture and philosophy share the world-outlook of a particular culture and time. Thus, early medieval philosophy has been said to explain much of early medieval Gothic architecture.

Places made Sacred by Formal Dedication

Almost any activity that imposes itself upon the ground requires a process of 'dedication' to that activity. Often the process is mundane: to build a factory requires land to be bought and planning permission sought. Generally, however, the 'higher' the activity the more elaborate the process of dedication. Town Halls, hospitals and schools all tend to have elaborate opening ceremonies; Victorian chapels frequently boasted a whole series of foundation stones, and specific dedication services and feasts were held.

Where sacred places are set apart for the regular performance of religious rites, most faiths provide some form of dedication ceremony. The Hindu temple is intended to be a conduit between God and humankind, which it achieves by offering the god a home or resting-place in his or her statue in the inner sanctum. Through the symbolism of its design and its holy purpose, the temple becomes not only the location of worship, but the object of worship. Crucial to its function is dedication. A series of rituals accompany the selection of the site, the drawing out of the temple's plan on the ground, the laying of the foundation stone, the final completion of the building and the installation of the principal *murti*.

After Christianity became the official religion of the Roman Empire, special dedication rites were developed for new churches. In Rome this was at first simply a mass said by the bishop, though later it became normal to deposit relics in the altar at the same time. In contrast to this funeral model, a much more elaborate rite developed in France based on the model of baptism, the main feature being the sprinkling of the church, inside and out, with holy water mixed with wine, salt and ashes. It also included a strange ceremony – which may perhaps be Irish in origin – in which the bishop used his staff to trace out the alphabet in ashes on the floor, in the shape of a great X, from corner to corner of the church. By the Middle Ages these two traditions had fused, so that the rite comprised the sprinkling of the church exterior, the bishop's entry, the alphabet ceremony, the sprinkling of the church interior, the deposition of relics in the altar, the consecration of the altar, and the mass. This elaborate rite lasted until the 1970s.

Places Made Sacred by the Presence of a Sacred Object

We have already discussed how the statue of the god in an Indian temple, when it is 'inhabited' by the god, can imbue the whole temple – the whole city – with its holiness. In a similar way, the presence of a holy person, or the body or relic of a holy person, can imbue a church or temple, and a much wider area as well, with its blessing and sanctity. Relics have played a crucial role in the development of Catholic and Orthodox Christianity, in Buddhism, and to some degree also in Islam.

Detail of wrought-iron gate at Tyntesfield Chapel.

The early Christians soon subverted the strict Roman rules against burial inside the city walls, because they had adopted the idea that virtue was catching and could be carried not only in dead bodies but in parts of bodies and inanimate objects. Everyone wanted to be able to visit a saint, to catch his or her virtue by touching the body with a piece of cloth, and to be buried nearby. As Christianity spread, rules forbidding the dismemberment of bodies were also overturned, and before long it became compulsory for altars to contain a relic, normally a fragment of a saint's body.

Such a relic imbued not just the altar but the whole church with its sanctity, and larger relics began to attract devotees and to perform miracles. Soon the idea of the wonder-working object extended to certain statues, the relic trade boomed, and the whole elaborate medieval economy of relics and pilgrimage blossomed (*see* Pilgrimage, p.56).

The Function of Sacred Places

Sacred places are useful – otherwise they would not exist. They provide a range of benefits and functions to the communities that 'run' them. One of the most common is healing: physical, mental and spiritual. Makasutu is a 500-hectare (202-acre) piece of bush in The Gambia. No hunting or fishing is allowed there; it is used exclusively for prayer and for rites of circumcision. Protected by myths featuring the hidden crown and clothes of a king, and a hidden paradise, it offers spiritual renewal for the individual, the protection of the community's rites of passage, and an effective nature reserve. Perhaps a landscape protected by the National Trust – with its link from past tradition to conservation for future generations – brings some similar benefits?

More overt is the healing offered by many shrines, where devotees seek, in return for their devotion and offerings, a cure for illness, successful childbirth, or a worldly advantage like business success, an exam pass, or an advantageous marriage. The strips of cloth often found tied to the branches of trees at holy wells and other sacred sites reflect the enduring traditional belief that, drawing on the energy of the place, as the fabric disintegrated, so would the illness or trouble, and healing would occur. One of the places where this can be seen is in the Chalice Well Garden, situated at the foot of Glastonbury Tor, and visited today by pilgrims of all faiths who believe that the reddish-tinged natural spring water to be found there has healing powers.

Sacred places have, too, a crucial political role. They frequently act as the symbol and focus of a community, whether that community is a village, a sect, a nation, or any other. And because they can easily act as such a symbol, they readily become contested, like Ayudhia or Jerusalem, or are deliberately targeted by the enemy, as so many such sites were in the wars in former Yugoslavia.

The National Trust is sometimes criticised for allowing its properties to become symbols that reinforce a conservative view of Britain. Sacred places can similarly take on a covert political role, either by becoming

The Lion's Head spring in the Chalice Well Garden, Glastonbury. It is also known as the Red or Blood spring because of the reddish coloration of the water.

symbols of a ruling class, or more subtly by becoming false symbols of a community's cohesion. In dividing the Buddha's relics into 84,000 pieces and distributing them throughout his empire, the great third-century emperor of India, Ashoka, was imposing his rule as well as his religion. But equally, sacred places can become the symbol of popular resistance to a regime, as the shrine at Czestochova did in communist Poland.

In identifying the different kinds of sacred place, we have perhaps discovered that what really matters is the difference in the way people look at sacred places: there are those who believe that 'sacredness' can really inhere in a particular piece of earth, and those who confess that 'it's only words' – that a place is only 'sacred' because we agree to call it so. Yet sacred places matter to us all because they offer the possibility of spiritual renewal for some. They matter to us all because, through understanding some of the traditions associated with these beliefs and empathising with them, we can all in part share in that renewal.

Waterfall at Hayburn Wyke, Yorkshire. The idea of spirits living in springs and streams was present again in the early twentieth-century fashion for 'fairies'. In November 1921 a member of the Theosophical Society believed he had seen, in a Lake District waterfall: a 'figure, which shines as if wet, is female, nude and without wings, the exquisite limbs gleam through the white auric flow, the arms are particularly long and beautiful, and she waves them gracefully in her flight'.

AVEBURY

In the Neolithic period – between 4500 and 2000BCE – the land that is now England was a landscape of elaborate ritual and great ceremonial monuments. This was the era when farming was first developing, and it seems very likely that it was to mark the territory of groups organised for agriculture, and to celebrate the power of an emerging aristocracy, that much of the ceremonial landscape was created.

Avebury was one of the greatest of the many distinct com-plexes of monuments in England. It lies today in the gentle north Wiltshire countryside at the headwater of the River Kennet, only 20 miles from Stonehenge. At its centre is the great 'henge' of Avebury itself, 400 metres across and with a hundred standing stones. It is now thought that the earthwork was built in phases, beginning before 2900BCE. Later, the massive 'sarsen' stones were brought from the nearby downs and set up inside the monument, possibly between 2600BCE and 2200BCE. This is the monument, still partly covered by the houses and gardens of the village, that most visitors come to see.

The henge itself, however, is only part of this great ceremonial complex. Two avenues, lined with standing stones, curl east and west from the henge. The eastern avenue ends at the timber and stone circles of the 'Sanctuary', while the recently rediscovered western one ends in an enigmatic ditched enclosure and 'cove' of standing stones. The whole mon-

ument is thus 4 kilometres (2½ miles) long. Just south of Avebury itself is Silbury Hill, the largest man-made mound in Europe. Excavation of the hill did not reveal human remains or treasure, and its intended purpose is unknown – suggested theories include a representation of a sacred mountain, or even a kind of viewing platform for those excluded from the henge itself during ceremonies.

above: William Stukeley's sketch of the Sanctuary made on 8 July 1723, shortly before it was destroyed. In the background can be seen Silbury Hill, with Windmill Hill and the village of Abury (Avebury).

Nearby is West Kennet long barrow; up to a thousand years before the building of Avebury, the bones of some fifty people were deposited here, sorted and stacked in five chambers. The tomb was modified, filled and finally blocked by a massive stone at the time that Avebury was being built. Also part of this extraordinary ceremonial landscape are Windmill Hill causewayed enclosure, already ancient when the Avebury stone circles were being erected, the palisade enclosures at West Kennet, and numerous other burial mounds.

The monuments of the Avebury complex were neglected for millennia: even knocked down, ploughed up, and built over. Rediscovered by the antiquaries of the seventeenth and eighteenth centuries – notably John Aubrey who, in 1648, put forward the theory that it was a Druid temple – the stone circle was drastically 'restored' by Alexander Keiller, heir to the Dundee Marmalade fortune, in the 1930s. He demolished many of the village houses that had been built within the circle, dug up and re-erected buried stones, and laid out a large part of the site for visitors. The 'timeless atmosphere' so enjoyed by visitors today is his creation.

The view from Windmill Hill.

above: The central circle of sarsen stones with bank and ditch enclosure. Avebury Manor is in the background.

Recent research has shown that the Avebury and Stonehenge groups were probably just the largest and most impressive of dozens, if not hundreds, of such ritual complexes in Neolithic England.

What were they for? Despite 'over 300 years of often heated debate, research and speculation' (as the archaeologists working recently at Avebury put it) we know very little about why they were built or how they were used. Recent theories emphasise ritual and agriculture. The structure and sheer size of the site indicate that large gatherings were held here – most likely to revere the dead, but also perhaps to celebrate festivals intended to ensure the 'return' of warmth and the sun each year. For each generation of farming families, what matters is the land, the seasons and the weather, and what their ancestors have done to create a productive farm. Perhaps this last concern could help explain why they set aside spare land on the boundaries between groups for ritual activities, to manage the relationship between the living and the dead.

Were these ceremonial landscapes 'sacred'? They may not have been 'religious', in the sense we use the word, at all. But they were clearly very special; at the very beginning of our society someone was willing to use a huge amount of resources – especially human muscle – to create a landscape that expressed their beliefs and hopes.

above: Aerial view of Avebury with the village at the centre.

Castlerigg in Cumbria is not only one of the most complete stone circles in Britain, and in the most beautiful setting, it is also possibly the earliest, built around 3000BCE.

BORROWDALE

Yew trees, especially big old ones, have generated much specualtion. In some ways they too are sacred places; perhaps the nearest we get in Britain to 'sacred groves'. Certainly they are often mysterious objects.

The yew tree attracts all sorts of local myths and legends. Perhaps the fact that it is poisonous, as well as dark, contributes to its association with death. Its habit of growing shoots or branches, which root themselves in the ground and grow to form a new trunk, perhaps contributes to the yew tree's role as a symbol of resurrection. Its longevity and ever-greenness perhaps leads to its use as a symbol of everlasting life.

It is difficult to tell how old yew trees are, because of their tendency to decay from the inside. As a result it is seldom possible to count their annual growth rings, or to use carbon14 dating. Some of the wilder guesses can be dis-counted, but most specialists agree that at least a few yew trees may well be over 1,500 years old.

In England ancient yews are particularly associated with church-yards, which probably contain several hundred yews of more than 800 years of age. Nobody really knows why that is. The 'yew-wood for long-bows' theory seems to be discounted: medieval longbows were made from imported Spanish yew. In Wales yews seem to be particularly associated with holy wells, and one unlikely theory suggests that yews mark the site of early saints' homes.

The Borrowdale Yews in Cumbria are still magnificent in decay, but they are wrecks com-pared to what they were when Wordsworth knew them as:

> … those fraternal Four of Borrowdale,
> Joined in one solemn and capacious grove;
> Huge trunks! and each particular trunk a growth
> Of intertwisted fibres serpentine
> Up-coiling, and inveterately convolved;
> Nor uninformed with Phantasy, and looks
> That threaten the profane;—a pillared shade,
> Upon whose grassless floor of red-brown hue,
> By sheddings from the pining umbrage tinged
> Perennially—beneath whose sable roof
> Of boughs, as if for festal purpose decked
> With unrejoicing berries—ghostly Shapes
> May meet at noontide; Fear and trembling Hope,
> Silence and Foresight; Death the Skeleton
> And Time the Shadow;—there to celebrate,
> As in a natural temple scattered o'er
> With altars undisturbed of mossy stone,
> United worship; or in mute repose
> To lie, and listen to the mountain flood
> Murmuring from Glaramara's inmost caves.

right: The largest of the 'Fraternal Four' yews at Borrowdale, Cumbria.

pages 38/39: The tranquil yew garden, based on the Sermon on the Mount, at Packwood House, Warwickshire.

CHEDWORTH ROMAN VILLA

Chedworth Roman Villa is one of the largest and best known of the great villas, or country houses, that dominated the peaceful agricultural landscape of this prosperous area of Roman Britain. Chedworth is famous for the elaborate mosaics that made its principal rooms so elegant, and for its unusually large bath house. The water comes from a natural spring on the edge of the site, which still runs.

The spring was led in the early fourth century into an eight-sided basin within an apsidal building, in which Victorian excavators found an uninscribed stone altar, and the base of a statue. This was very probably a nymphaeum, or temple to the goddess (nymph) of the spring. Later villa owners, though, may well have been Christian, because at some stage *chi-rhos* (symbols of Christ) were scratched into the stone rim of the basin.

In Greek and Roman mythology, hills, forests, caves, springs and streams all had their nymphs, imagined as eternally beautiful young girls, who would dance with Dionysus or hunt with Artemis, while many other gods were fascinated by them. The nymph Daphne was pursued by Apollo in a famous myth, while it was the beautiful sea-nymph Calypso who detained the hero Odysseus on her island.

They were friendly towards mortals, and water-nymphs, in particular, were rich in favours and encouraged fruitfulness in plants, animals and mortals. Indeed, they tended to fall in love with men. So they were invoked to bless marriages, and even in towns nymphaea were built as wedding-halls. Nymphs received offerings of goats, lambs, milk and oil.

However, it has recently been suggested that perhaps Chedworth is not a Villa at all, but a temple complex. It has been argued that this is an awkward site for a country house and farm, and many of the excavated buildings seem more easily interpreted as temples, dormitories for pilgrims and bath houses for ritual baths, than as domestic and farm buildings. Comparisons have been made with the hilltop shrine to Nodens at Lydney in Gloucestershire, with the urban shrine of Sulis Minerva at Bath, and with other major Roman healing centres in Germany and France.

right: The west wing of Chedworth Roman Villa, showing the mosaic floor of the Tepidarium (Warm Room) and semi-circular hot bath.

below: The Nymphaeum.

CLANDON PARK

One meaning of 'sacred' is 'set apart', usually for the service of God, or for some religious purpose. The Maori people of New Zealand inherit from their Pacific island ancestors a strong concept of *tapu*, by which certain persons, places or things were sacred or – alternatively – unclean or forbidden. For example, in some respects a house is *tapu*, and therefore cooked food is never eaten inside nor rainwater collected from the roof. A burial ground is *tapu*, but then so used to be a warrior about to go into battle. For Maoris who value their traditions, anyone who violates *tapu* puts themselves in great danger, and elaborate rites are needed to lift *tapu* from a person or object.

Also from their Pacific past the Maori inherited the tradition of a village square, the *marae*, which was the focus of the tribe or sub-tribe's social life. On one side of the square there is generally a formal gateway, on the other the Meeting House or *whare nui*. Such Meeting Houses serve many of the functions met in an English village by the church, inn or village hall. They are used for funerals, meetings of all sorts, and concerts, as well as to put up visitors. In the later nineteenth century they became much bigger than they had been, and Maori leaders built Meeting Houses as a political and cultural statement. They became the focus for the revival of Maori woodcarving and craftwork, but also of Maori self-expression and self-confidence.

Not only is the Meeting House usually named after the founding ancestor of the tribe, it is conceived as the ancestor him- or herself. The carved or painted barge-boards represent his outstretched arms, the ridgepole his back, and the rafters his ribs. Thus a meeting of the tribe takes place in the bosom of the ancestor, surrounded by carvings of the gods, legendary heroes and ancestors, as well as, today, by photographs of distinguished tribal members.

The remarkable Maori House at Clandon Park is of the earliest of the surviving Meeting Houses, the only one in Britain, and surely the one with the most extraordinary history. It was built in 1880, by the popular and entrepreneurial sub-tribe leader Aporo, in New Zealand's first tourist village. The village of Te Wairo was then the centre of what is still New Zealand's principal tourist area, and then, as now, tourists came to see both the volcanic hot springs and lakes, and the local Maori life. Aporo planned his new building to be a Meeting House for local people, but also to be a tourist centre where – for a fee – visitors could see Maori *haka* and other dance performances. He named it after Hinemihi, a noted female chief of some 250 years earlier.

Eight years later, disaster struck. The sacred mountain Tarawera – an 'extinct' volcano – erupted, causing devastation for miles around; 500sq.km (193 sq.miles) was covered with dust and mud up to 22m (72ft) deep. The village of Te Wairo disappeared, and the only surviving building was the new Meeting House, Hinemihi.

When the Governor General of New Zealand let it be known that he wanted to acquire a Meeting House to take home to Britain as a souvenir, his attention was drawn to the abandoned and derelict Hinemihi. Lord Onslow bought her for £50, and shipped her home to his family seat at Clandon Park, where she was

rebuilt as a boat house beside the lake. Another change of fortune came in 1917, when Clandon Park was a military convalescent hospital, and soldiers from the Maori Pioneer Battalion moved Hinemihi nearer the house, and restored her nearer to her original form – though she remained for many years little more than a garden shed. After the National Trust took over Clandon Park in 1956 there were a number of attempts at restoration, as well as requests for her return to New Zealand.

In 1986 Hinemihi received new recognition when a Maori performance group toured Britain to promote New Zealand tourism. They asked to visit Clandon Park, and the organiser Alan Gallop recalls the visit:

As the group climbed out in their smart red and black Maori Arts and Crafts Institute uniforms, we sensed unease among them. Missing were the smiles and good-natured rapport established earlier on the road. Instead everyone was serious and in no mood for joking.

We... stood in silence as we looked across the garden towards the small wooden house. After a pause Emily let out a loud cry as if calling to

someone inside the building. ... Other cries came from elsewhere in the group as they walked slowly towards the building. As we drew nearer still we noticed many were weeping.

The group came to a standstill about 4m away from Hinemihi and stood in silence. Suddenly, and without warning, the door flew open. None of us were aware that anyone was inside and we could see through the window and doorway that the building was empty.

Later the group leader explained:

...we could feel the presence of our ancestors, including those who sheltered inside Hinemihi during the eruption, as well as those who didn't make it to safety. By touching the carvings we could hear their screams, feel their pain.

This visit led to others, and eventually to the full restoration of the Meeting House, by craftsmen and wood-carvers from the Maori Arts and Crafts Institute, based only a few miles from the site of Te Wairo.

The meeting house... is highly *tapu* in the sacred sense. Respect for the sanctity of the

house is marked by the custom of removing shoes before entering, and by the prohibition of food inside. The house, with its carvings of gods, culture heroes and ancestors, is the analogue to a cathedral. It is the celestial realm, the domain of peace and harmony...

As you step into the porch, you pass from this world to the other. On either side of Hinemihi's porch, and on the apex of her roof, are elaborate carvings, probably of ancestors, while over the door is carved Tane, oldest child of Papatuanuka, (Earth Mother) and Ranginui (Sky Father), separating his parents and creating light between earth and sky – the Maori story of Creation. Inside, the central column carries carvings of Hinemihi's ancestor Ngatoro-irangi, priest of the Te Arawa canoe which brought the original members of the tribe from Hawaiki 1,000 years before, and of her legendary pet giant lizard, Kataore.

The original carving was done by two of the greatest of all Maori carvers, Wero Taroi and Tene Waitere. For Maori people, all carvings have a life – *mana* – of their own, and are seen as living things, rather as in Europe a boat is seen by sailors.

FARNE ISLANDS

The Farne Islands are one of the most exciting places in Britain for the naturalist. With over 70,000 pairs of nesting birds, the islands are famous for the swirling clouds of puffins which in July are preparing to leave for the Atlantic, the huge colonies of Guillemots and shags covering the rocky volcanic cliffs, and the grey seals which bask on the rocks and bob up to greet visiting boats. Most visitors to Inner Farne today spend only an hour on the island, as part of a boat tour of the Farne Islands from the Northumberland resort of Seahouses. But even in an hour one can sense what a special place it is.

The Farne Islands are forever linked with the name of one of northern England's most famous – and attractive – saints: Cuthbert. St Cuthbert was born to well-to-do Anglo-Saxon parents, and became a monk at the monastery of Melrose in 651. He was obviously a man of huge charm and energy, for he was elected prior ten years later, and earned a reputation for undertaking missionary campaigns in the surrounding countryside. This was the time when the church in northern England was struggling to reconcile the traditions it had received from Ireland with those of Rome, a dilemma symbolised by the argument over the date of Easter. Eventually the Roman faction won, and Cuthbert, newly-elected prior of Lindisfarne, had the job of persuading the monks to accept the new ideas.

Besides energy and political skills, Cuthbert also had a deep spirituality, firmly in the traditions of the Celtic church. Celtic spirituality, and especially its particular concern with nature, appeals to people of the twenty-first century just as it did to those of the seventh. Like so many of the early saints, Cuthbert had a particular relationship with animals. The Venerable Bede, a Northumbrian monk and scholar who wrote Cuthbert's biography thirty years after his death, records how two otters once came to warm Cuthbert's feet after a night praying in the sea, and how a sea eagle gave him a fish when he was hungry.

After some ten years as prior, Cuthbert took himself off to a hermitage on the nearby un-inhabited island of Inner Farne (*right*). There he built himself a round hut of stones and turf and straw thatch, planted barley, and lived alone for ten years, be-coming more and more withdrawn and indifferent to 'the world'. He grew to ignore visitors – even his fellow monks who came to bring him food – but would talk to the birds. When he told off a flock of birds for raiding his barley crop 'all the flock of birds departed, and never more returned to feed upon that field', and a pair of crows who had taken straw from his thatch for their nests:

...flew away in sorrow. At the end of three days one of the two returned, and finding the man of God digging in the field, spread its wings in a pitiable manner, and bending its head down before his feet, in a tone of humility asked pardon by the most expressive signs it could, and obtained from the reverend father permission to return.

So famous did Cuthbert become that he was elected bishop of Lindisfarne, but it took the pleading of the king himself to persuade him to leave Inner Farne. As bishop his reputation for holiness, preaching, prophecies and miracles of healing grew even greater, but after only two years he sensed he was dying and returned to his hermitage, where he died two months later, in 687. The Farne Islands have been remembered as Cuthbert's home ever since, and the ubiquitous Eider Duck is still known after him as the 'Cuddy Duck'.

One of Cuthbert's successors was the hermit Bartholomew. One

day he was at prayer in the chapel when he felt a duck tugging at his cloak. He followed her, and came to a crevice in the rock; looking in, he saw a duckling trapped at the bottom. Bartholomew, of course, climbed down, rescued the duckling and gave it back to its mother 'who in high delight seemed by her joyous look to give him thanks. Whereupon she took to the water with her sons, and Bartholomew, dumb with astonishment, went back to his oratory'.

During the later Middle Ages the island was wardened by two monks from Durham; in 1307 they were growing three acres of barley, and kept a bull, two cows, a horse, a pig, four sheep, six capons, six hens and a cock. They also killed seals for their oil and blubber, and supplied porpoise and seal meat to the Durham monastery. After the Dissolution of the Monasteries the islands had a succession of tenants who came to exploit their wildlife, for eggs, feathers, food or oil. In 1848 an Anglican clergyman, Archdeacon Charles Thorpe, took a lease on the islands and began, by employing 'watchers', to safeguard their unique wildlife. He also restored one of the two medieval chapels. In doing so he added yet another strand of spirituality to Farne's heritage, for he placed in the restored chapel furnishings rescued from Durham Cathedral. These had been installed in the cathedral by Bishop John Cosin after the restoration of Charles II, and their remarkable mixture of Baroque and Gothic styles reflect something of Cosin's High Church views, and his desire to restore beauty to worship.

Sunset over Seahouses, on the Northumberland coast. Boats carrying visitors to the Farne Islands depart from here.

above: *King Egfrid Landing on the Farne Islands to Summon Cuthbert to Become a Bishop*, by William Bell Scott (1811–90). From the murals in the Central Hall at Wallington, Northumberland. The 'Cuddy Duck' is at Cuthbert's side.

GIANT'S CAUSEWAY

above: 'The Organ' rock formation at the Giant's Causeway.

In the north of Ireland there once lived a giant called Fionn Mac Cumhail, Finn MacCool. He was around fifty feet tall, but across the sea in Scotland lived a much bigger giant. Finn MacCool rashly challenged his rival to a trial of strength, and to make the contest possible he built a rocky causeway between the two countries, from County Antrim to the rival's lair – Fingal's Cave on the island of Staffa.

Finn was so exhausted by his work he fell heavily asleep. The next morning Oonagh, Finn's giantess wife, woke to thunderous footsteps, saw the Scottish giant approaching, and realised that Finn could never stand up to him. She quickly covered the still-sleeping Finn with a nightgown and bonnet. The Scottish giant peered in at the door. 'Shhhh', said Oonagh, 'or you'll wake the baby'. The Scottish rival thought, 'If their baby is this big, how big must Finn be?'. He rushed back across the causeway, destroying it as he went, leaving only the ends in Ireland and on Staffa.

What is it that prompts people to associate legends of giants and heroes, goblins and battles, with particular places? Sometimes, as at the Giant's Causeway, the answer seems obvious – to explain the strange character of the place. Elsewhere the reason is less clear, and must lie in people's need to make their own place seem special, to themselves and to others. Sometimes, perhaps there is genuinely a muddled folk memory of battles or treasure.

Ireland's north-east coast is a landscape of dramatic cliffs, romantic ruins, seabirds and sea-spray. At one point there rises up the cliffs from the sea an extraordinary geological formation, where enormous quantities of basalt have cooled into thousands of polygonal columns, looking like so many giant organ pipes. It seems they cannot possibly be natural. This is the Giant's Causeway, and it has its equivalent in a similar formation just across the North Channel in Fingal's Cave on the Scottish island of Staffa.

GLASTONBURY TOR

Glastonbury Tor has a remarkable shape, rising out of the Somerset Levels and visible from miles away. It is easy to see why it is thought by some to represent one breast of the Goddess, whose figure forms the Glastonbury landscape, marking the centre of ancient fertility religion, the entrance to fairyland, and a three-dimensional maze.

The Tor is a 325m (1100ft) conical hill on the edge of this Somerset market town, which over the past half-century has become one of the world's great centres of alternative spirituality, or New Age religion. It may perhaps attract today as many pilgrims as it did when the great medieval abbey was standing. Glastonbury is thought of as the Isle of Avalon, the site of a great Druidic centre of learning, a centre of prehistoric Goddess worship, the 'cradle of English Christianity', visited by Joseph of Arimathea after the Crucifixion, the 'New Jerusalem', a communication point for alien contact, the 'epicentre' of New Age in England, the 'heart chakra' of planet earth.

People today move easily from one cult to another, choosing what has meaning for them. Paganism, Celtic Christianity, Goddess worship, Wicca and others all share an emphasis on the preciousness, power and vulnerability of the Earth. New Age religion, with its variety of beliefs, cults and practices, has refocused attention on sacred places. The concept of Gaia – the Earth as a living being – has gone hand-in-hand with the idea that the Earth, like the human body, has lines of energy. These 'ley-lines', through which the Earth's energy flows almost like a National Grid, pass through significant points, often represented on the ground by ancient monuments or churches, and these are places of power. Glastonbury is seen as one of the principal nodes in the Earth's energy grid.

At the top of the Tor are the remains of a medieval church dedicated to the Archangel Michael (see p.84). It was here that at the time of the Dissolution of the Monasteries Richard Whiting, the last Abbot of Glastonbury, was hanged for defying King Henry VIII. At its foot is the Chalice Well (see p.26), a natural spring whose high chalybeate content has given it its reputation for healing, and where some believe Joseph of Arimathea hid the Holy Grail – the Chalice of the Last Supper. In the nearby abbey ruins the monks claimed to have found the grave of King Arthur, while beside the Parish Church is a thorn tree which, it is sometimes claimed, is descended from the thorn that sprouted from Joseph of Arimathea's staff.

Traditional formal religion has become rare in twenty-first century Western Europe, but personal spirituality is surely as strong as ever. A Christian minister told a researcher that in Glastonbury people tend to ask, 'What is your truth?' rather than, 'What is the truth?'. For most people, the answer would include some reference to the sacred place.

top left: The Glastonbury Thorn.

GREYS COURT

I had a dream of a maze. There were some people very close to the centre, but they could not find a way through. Just outside the maze others were standing. They were further away from the heart of the maze, but they would be there sooner than the party that fretted and fumed inside. I long to be able to speak, while Archbishop, with men and women who stand outside the Christian Church. I would say to them: 'You can teach us so much if together we could look for the secret of the maze-like muddle in which the world finds itself.'

Listening, as Archbishop Robert Runcie gave his inaugural address in 1980, was someone who had been mulling over the idea of adding a real maze to the gardens she was creating around the historic family home. Just nine months later the Archbishop came and dedicated the 'Archbishop's Maze' at Greys Court in Oxfordshire.

Designed for Lady Elizabeth Brunner by the leading modern maze-designers, Adrian Fisher and Randoll Coate, the Archbishop's Maze is replete with Christian symbolism. In one sense the maze is a puzzle, with choices to be made at each of the cruciform junctions. By following the true path, however, and crossing straight over each of the diamond-shaped thorns, one walks the whole quarter-mile without once retracing one's steps. This route is the Path of Life. Although the path brings one within sight of Salvation – close to the centre – it remains out of reach, for Death intervenes, and the path turns away from the centre and winds its way back to the outer circle again. From there it leads at last to the heart of the maze, to the beginning of Eternal Life.

The details of the maze are equally full of symbolism. The overall design comprises the crown of thorns, in paths made of bricks laid out in cruciform pattern. The seven rings of the crown represent the seven days of Creation. The turf centre of the maze measures nine times the width of the turf between the brick paths, and recalls Christ's nine hours of agony. At the centre are two crosses, a simple Roman cross of Bath stone within an elaborate Byzantine cross of blue West-moreland stone; they proclaim the reconciliation between East and West, Catholic and Protestant, Roman and Orthodox. Finally, at the very centre is a pillar inscribed with lines from Saint Augustine, Julian of Norwich, Siegfried Sassoon and Robert Gittings, and bearing an armillary sundial, 'which places the visitor at an exact point in space and time, in the middle of this maze whose message is timeless'.

Not all mazes, by any means, are intended to have religious symbolism; many modern ones are merely ornamental, or just for fun, and probably many ancient ones were too. At least eight National Trust properties contain mazes; Glendurgan Garden in Cornwall, for example, has a laurel maze created in 1833 by the owner to amuse his children. Yet labyrinths (mazes with only one route) have seen a big revival as spiritual tools in recent years, in both Christian and New Age contexts. Mostly these are based on the design of the famous labyrinth laid about 1202 on the floor of Chartres cathedral, and are meant to be walked along in meditation, or contemplated as a symbol of the spiritual path. The Chartres pattern

is the classic medieval design, followed too by most old labyrinths in Britain, as well as by other cathedral and church labyrinths in France and elsewhere. Whether these were really 'paths to Jerusalem', followed by pilgrims on their knees, is unknown; the one at Auxerre was the focus of a liturgical Easter circle-dance by the cathedral's priests, but the one at Reims was destroyed in 1779 because children playing on it disturbed the cathedral services.

HAILES ABBEY

Pilgrimage is a phenomenon found in every age, every culture and every religion, from Sikhism to Buddhism, from Hindu India to Moslem Africa, and from ancient Greece to modern France. Pilgrimage is one of the most obvious ways in which religion relates to landscape. Typically, having received a blessing on leaving home, the pilgrim joins a band of others for the journey. This might be a group on foot or horseback, as Chaucer describes, or a modern coach party, but the atmosphere of expectancy and camaraderie, frivolity and devotion will be the same. Anthropologists draw attention to the importance of this in-between stage in the pilgrim's experience, and for many the journey is at least as important as the experience at the shrine itself.

One of the most popular destinations in medieval England was Hailes Abbey in Gloucestershire, where pilgrims could adore the very blood shed for them by their Saviour. A few drops of Christ's blood in a small phial were exhibited in an elaborate shrine behind the High Altar.

Pilgrims came in their thousands, from every part of England and from every level of society. As Bishop Hugh Latimer put it, 'I dwell within half a mile of the Fossway, and you would wonder to see how they come by flocks out of the west country to many images, but chiefly to the blood of Hales'. One pilgrim was the awkward, talkative, much-travelled visionary from King's Lynn, Margery Kempe, who came in 1417: 'there she was shriven and had loud cries and boisterous weepings. Then the religious men had her in amongst them and made her good cheer' (but characteristically she told them off roundly for swearing). Chaucer's Pardoner condemned swearing 'by the blood of Crist that is in Hayles'.

They came, as all pilgrims come, for a great variety of reasons: some out of devotion to Christ, many to seek healing, some to fulfil a penance, some as another step on the way of a wandering hermit. Many came for more secular reasons: to have an adventure or to escape from difficulties at home. No doubt most pilgrims to Hailes, as elsewhere, came out of a mixture of motives, but all would hope to be changed for the better by the experience.

They entered the church by the north transept, and turned left to make their way round the specially built pilgrim route around the east end of the church. In the centre, behind the high altar, stood the great shrine.

In the earlier Middle Ages most pilgrimages were to saints' shrines, but later shrines to Christ or his mother Mary became more popular. Today Christian pilgrimage in Europe is dominated by great centres like Lourdes in France, Knock in Ireland and Medjugorge in Bosnia, where Mary appeared in person to ordinary people.

Little remains today of the church and monastery at Hailes Abbey. The phial of the Holy Blood itself was finally destroyed, on 24 November 1539 at St Paul's Cross in London, by the Bishop of Rochester who claimed it 'to be no blood, but honey clarified and coloured with saffron'.

opposite right: *St James with a Donor*, attributed to Rogier Van der Weyden (1399–1464), in the dining room at Petworth House, Sussex. The painting depicts St James as a Christian pilgrim.

below: The story of Exodus is read from the Haggadah at every Passover meal. Passover is one of the three great pilgrimage festivals of Judaism, but since the destruction of the Temple, the ritual now takes place at home. This Haggadah, from the library at Blickling Hall, Norfolk, is one of the finest eighteenth-century Jewish manuscripts.

HOLYSTONE

'Holy Wells' are common through-out the British Isles. Some are named after saints, or are associated with them in local tradition, reflecting the notion that the wells were often said to have appeared spontaneously as a result of the prayers of a particular saint. Some were regarded into Victorian times – and in some cases, even today – as having healing powers. Passers-by would drop coins or bent pins into the water, or tie rags (known as 'clouties' in Scotland) to nearby bushes and trees, 'for luck' and in the hope that the affliction would gradually disappear as the piece of cloth disintegrated. The old tradition of well-dressing, in which the wells are decorated with flower-pictures, was revived in the nineteenth century and now flourishes in Derbyshire and the Peak District. A few wells, most notably St Winefride's Well in North Wales, are formally adopted by the church and are the focus of regular services and bathing of the sick.

Lady Well, or 'The Lady's Well', at Holystone, Northumbria, is sometimes said to be the place where in the Easter of 627 the Roman missionary Paulinus baptised 3,000 Anglo-Saxons, including the Northumbrian King, Edwin: hence the Victorian statue of him beside it. Another, equally unlikely, legend associates it with St Ninian, the fifth-century bishop and apostle of Christianity in Scotland. In the Middle Ages it was in the care of a small house of Benedictine nuns in the village. Very little is known for certain about its history, but people were leaving pins in the well in the 1880s. Today the tranquility and beauty of its setting ensures that it is still visited as a special place.

Recently some have questioned the whole idea of the 'holy well', especially the romantic idea that holy wells represent the survival, under a thin Christian veneer, of very ancient pagan traditions in which water at its source represented a link to another world, and was regarded as a means of carrying prayers or offerings to the gods. Instead, they look at the different kinds of well separately. There are wells used for healing (which, as the source of natural spring water, may actually contain valuable minerals); wells featuring in popular customs; haunted wells; wells named after saints, and so on. Some (perhaps many, even most?) 'holy wells' were clearly so-called not because of any inherent sanctity but because they once belonged to a church or a monastery, while some that seem to be named after saints were really named after churches. This seems likely to be the case at Holystone, where Lady's Well belonged to the Priory of St Mary. Increasingly, too, studies are being made into how the ways in which wells have been used, named, and looked at, has changed over time. One major change has been the way in which the church, in the early centuries, vigorously condemned 'worship' of wells, but later came to welcome their popular veneration as a way of leading people to faith.

above: Lady's Well, Holystone.

opposite: The 'Holy Well' in the grounds of Lanhydrock, Cornwall, is probably one of the many 'holy wells' that got their name in Victorian times.

HOUSESTEADS FORT

Throughout the world, caves have been seen as places of very special significance, as gateways to the underworld, or birthplaces of the gods, or places of transformation. Where genuine caves are not available, they are sometimes replicated, for example in the grottoes of Our Lady of Lourdes, sometimes seen in the grounds of Roman Catholic churches. In a somewhat similar way, perhaps, temples of Mithras were built to give the feeling of caves.

Mithraism was a mystery religion practised for three centuries in the late Roman empire, and was particularly popular in the Roman army. It seems to have been strong in Britain, for Mithraea – temples of Mithras – have been found in London, but also especially on Hadrian's Wall. The one at Housesteads, Northumberland, lay among a group of temples and cemeteries beyond the civilian village that straggled down the hill from the Fort to the main road.

Mithras was born from the rock, it was from rock that light descended to earth, and he struck the rock to release life-giving water. It was in the cave that Mithras slew the bull, the central act that renewed life.

Mithraea reproduced much of this symbolism, for Mithraism offered its adherents salvation through involvement in the liturgy that reproduced the myth. Often built partly underground, at the west end was an entrance hall, and beyond that a windowless nave where, it seems, worshippers burned incense, sang hymns, and shared the meal that commemorated the one Mithras himself had shared with the sun-god Sol. At the east end, the sanctuary replicated the cave, and through the gloom and the smoke from incense burning on the altars, worshippers could glimpse the great painted relief of Mithras slaying the bull.

Mithras was the mediator between the unapproachable and unknowable God in heaven, and suffering humanity, and his conquest of the bull was the symbol of human triumph over suffering. He called his faithful followers to a life of struggle for Good against Evil, but he offered them both immortality of the soul and resurrection of the flesh. Never a mass religion (the Housesteads temple probably only accommodated a couple of dozen worshippers), in Britain Mithraism was particularly popular with army officers and traders. Its seeming similarities to their own religion earned it the particular hatred of Christians, who eventually destroyed it.

above: A view from Housesteads Fort towards Beggar Bog.

right: Reconstruction of the Mithraeum found in the nearby Roman wall fort of Carrawburgh. The Housesteads temple was no doubt very similar.

KEDLESTON HALL

Islam relates in many ways to the landscape. One of the most obvious is the pilgrimage to Mecca, which sees two million Moslems crossing continents in the great annual pilgrimage. The city of Mecca is quintessentially a sacred place, its outer limits defined by stone markers, with the supremely sacred *Ka'aba* at its centre. Mecca is the focus of prayer, both personal and collective; every mosque has its *qibla* wall showing the direction of the holy city, and every Moslem bows in prayer towards Mecca five times a day.

Though not all Moslems think it orthodox, the tomb is a vital element in Islam as it has been practised by Caliph and commoner alike, and in many parts of the Moslem world cemeteries cluster round the tomb of the local saint. The living saint plays a key role in this popular Islam. People visit him – sometimes from far away – to seek his help and advice, or just to pay their respects. The *baraka* (blessing) he emanated in life continues to pour from his tomb in death. The tomb is his continuing home, so a saint or martyr is honoured with a building worthy to receive his guests. Such shrines continue the architectural form of ancient tombs, centrally planned – often square or octagonal – with the tomb itself in the centre, facing in the direction of Mecca.

But not only saints and martyrs lie in imposing tombs. While ordinary folk must be content with a simple earth grave and rough stone or wood marker, the wealthy and powerful have always tried to ensure their burial in imposing mausolea, often surrounded by a funerary garden. A tradition of splendid tombs grew up throughout the Islamic world, usually based on a domed, centrally planned, form. The square plinth may be seen as standing for the material universe; the dome for the circle of eternity; while the garden, divided into four quarters which are subdivided again by paths or runnels of water, represents paradise.

This tradition reached its peak in Moslem North India, and the Taj Mahal, completed by Shah Jehan (*c.*1592–1666) in 1653 for his favourite wife, is perhaps the most beautiful and splendid of all. This model, acquired by Lord Curzon when he was Viceroy of India (1898–1905), survives in his collection at Kedleston Hall, Derbyshire.

THE LAKE DISTRICT

The Lake District is still seen by many as England's spiritual landscape par excellence. Yet the Lake District is also the prime example of a landscape which we have created, by the assumptions and expectations that we bring when we visit it.

Earlier travellers had seen the Lakes simply as an unproductive countryside where travel was difficult; it was the Romantic painters and writers who pointed to the mountain landscape as picturesque, stupendous, awesome, noble. By the later eighteenth century gentlemen tourists in search of 'the picturesque' were beginning to look at the Lakes through eyes conditioned by the Grand Tour and classical landscapes. They saw the landscape as inspiring and exciting, but they did not yet see it as in any way spiritual. John Wesley said of a Lakeland congregation in 1759 that 'they found God to be a God both of the hills and valleys, and no where more present than in the mountains of Cumberland', and one editor comments 'it should be noted that when Wesley says that God is "nowhere more present than in the mountains of Cumberland", he is not anticipating Wordsworth. On the contrary, he is implying that these mountains were the last place where anyone would expect to find God!'

That the Lake District was in some sense a place of spiritual power was the discovery of the nineteenth century, and above all of Wordsworth. Here he is on Scafell:

> This is a temple built by God's own hand –
> Mountains its walls, its gorgeous roof the sky –
> Where uncontrolled the exalted soul partakes
> Her natural and high communion.
> Loses all thought of this world's pigmy pomp,
> And in the stern and distant solitude
> Feels as alone with the Invisible.

Wordsworth, the Cumbrian poet Norman Nicholson remarks, 'covered hill and dale, farm and inn, wagonette and picnic-basket, with the fat, yellow, comfortable warmth of religiosity', and accuses him of 'confusing the exhilaration of mountain climbing with the fervour of religious experience'. Yet it was Wordsworth who introduced English readers to the idea that landscape could be spiritual. The idea appealed strongly to the middle-class tourists who, in later Victorian times and since, flocked

Derwentwater and Skiddaw from the lakeshore at Kettlewell.

left: William Wordsworth's birthplace in Cockermouth, Cumbria. The garden runs down to the River Derwent, which is celebrated in *The Prelude*: 'the bright blue river passed/Along the margin of our walk'.
It was poets and painters who taught us to see the landscape as a spiritual resource. As the art historian Kenneth Clark put it: 'Both poet and painter found nature transformed by the philosophy of the eighteenth century into a mechanical universe working under the dictates of common sense; and both believed that there was something in trees, flowers, meadows and mountains which was so full of the divine that if it were contemplated with sufficient devotion it would reveal a moral and spiritual quality of its own.'

to the Lakes, and who now saw the landscape through Wordsworth's eyes, and who were and are only too glad to claim their holiday as good for the soul.

This view of the Lake District as a 'sacred place' was a real motive for the National Trust's acquisition of so much land there. Canon Hardwicke Rawnsley, one of the Trust's three founders, wrote these verses to celebrate the opening in 1902 of the National Trust's first Lake District land at Brandlehow Park on the banks of Derwentwater:

From such a hill might angels long to lean
And gaze once more upon their native place;
So calm the waters – Walla face to face
So calm – Blencathra, Skiddaw, so serene –
You scarce might think earth's central fires had been
The makers of this gentle mountain race

. . . .

And here may mortals, weary of the strife
Of inconsiderate cities, hope to come
And learn the fair tranquillities of earth;
Here men may pray, here poet-thoughts have birth,
Here all shy forest-creatures find a home,
And wild-wood pleasaunce help the Nation's life.

opposite: Derwentwater from the shore of Brandelhow Park, with Blencathra (Saddleback) in the far left distance.

LAVENHAM GUILDHALL

When in 1529 the Guild of Corpus Christi built its Guildhall, Lavenham in Suffolk was (thanks to the woollen trade) the fourteenth richest town in England, and the Guild seems to have comprised its leading citizens. Though its records have sadly been lost, the Guild no doubt took the lead in organising the Corpus Christi Day parade in Lavenham in early summer. There would be a great cross, children with garlands, candles, bells and flags, and the other Guilds with their banners. At its heart would be the Host, carried in a shrine by a priest, beneath a canopy of honour carried by the principal men of the town. They were declaring that the town belonged to Christ – but also, perhaps, to them.

Processions were a widely adopted custom in pre-modern society, and a useful tool for the city's dominant class. Such parades, often incorporating virtually all the men of the community, demonstrated both the organisation of society, and the ruling élite's control of space. It was a declaration that the streets and market places of the town belonged to them. These processions expressed the corporate order of urban society. They have been called 'a statement unfurled in the streets, through which the city represented itself to itself, and to God'.

Moreover, these parades represented God to the city. In medieval England they did so almost literally, for the great day for such processions was the feast of Corpus Christi, usually in early June, when the Host would be processed through the city. The parades declared at once that the city belonged to the ordered ranks of society and that it belonged to God. The city itself was declared to be a sacred place.

In most towns of any size the Guilds would organise feasts, Masses and elaborate parades, involving pageantry, splendid costumes, music, elaborate floats, and sometimes tableaux carried on wagons, or short 'mystery' plays put on at the various stopping places. The Guilds offered their members three things: in health, a fraternity reinforced by a lively social life; in sickness, distress or old age, relief and care; and after death, a worthy funeral and help for the soul through prayer and regular Masses. The great majority of the men of the town would belong to one of the Guilds and would take part in the processions, everyone dressed and placed according to his rank in society.

above: Detail of carving on the doorpost in Lavenham Guildhall.

LOUGHWOOD MEETING HOUSE

Jesus, where'er thy people meet,
There they behold thy mercy-seat;
Where'er they seek thee, thou art found,
And every place is hallowed ground.

For thou, within no walls confined,
Inhabitest the humble mind;
....

The hymn by the poet William Cowper expresses strongly the Protestant tradition of suspicion of holy places. God can be found anywhere: He lives in people's minds and hearts, not in buildings. This is the tradition that created the humble, vernacular nonconformist chapel.

This modest little chapel and Staunton Harold church (see p.94) were built at almost exactly the same time. Yet in their purpose, appearance and theology they are as different as two places of Christian worship well could be.

Loughwood Meeting House was built by Particular Baptists in the village of Kilmington on the Dorset/Devon border in 1653. The Baptists are one of the largest Protestant communions, notably strong today in the southern United States. They are distinguished by their belief that the Bible teaches that only adult believers should receive baptism, while Particular Baptists held that only the Elect – those chosen by God – would go to heaven. Baptists emerged in the early seventeenth century (John Bunyan was one of the most famous), and soon became associated with radical spiritual and political ideas. As a result they were persecuted by the authorities, and this Meeting House was founded in a deliberately remote spot, where the preachers could easily escape from the magistrates into the next county.

Loughwood Meeting House is one of the earliest surviving nonconformist chapels in the country. The furnishings may be rather later; they include pulpit, communion table and box pews, and the mark of a Baptist church, a baptism tank below the communion table. All must die to the old Adam and rise to new life with Christ through the waters of Baptism.

There is absolutely nothing 'churchy' about this building; its style is that of the smaller farmhouses of the district, and this no doubt represents the attitude of the early congregations. The chapel was a functional place for the encounter of believers with one another and with God. So transcendent and so momentous an experience made any decoration or ceremony quite redundant, so early chapels had 'the quality of a well-scrubbed farmhouse kitchen', as John Betjeman put it.

MOUNT GRACE PRIORY

The wellspring of our Carthusian life is divine love, and the goal of our lives is divine love...The rhythm of modern life is so feverish, agitated and clamorous that the majority of people have to re-educate themselves in order to recover a rhythm that is in harmony with a deepening interior life. Stillness, silence, peace have to be learnt (Lockhart, 1999).

Carthusian monks today still share the mystical spirituality that, in the later Middle Ages, was one of the principal inspirations of lay piety.

right: Reconstruction of the living room of a Carthusian monk's cell.

The Order was founded in 1084 by St Bruno, in the French Alpine valley of Grande Chartreuse, from which it took its name.

Deliberately modelling themselves on the early Christian desert hermits, the Carthusians sought union with God through silence, solitude, fasting, meditation and continual prayer. For the Carthusian monk, his cell was both heaven, where at any time he might be favoured with the Beatific Vision and the sense of intimate union with God, and a battlefield on which he fought the devil. The Carthusians remained austere,

devout and respected until the very end, when some of them were martyred for their resistance to King Henry VIII. Today there are some 400 Carthusian monks and nuns, in 24 houses across Europe and the Americas, including one in Sussex and one in Vermont.

Mount Grace Priory, in North Yorkshire, was founded in the later fourteenth century. Each of the 20 monks lived in his own little house, with its own tiny lobby, living room, bedroom/oratory, upstairs workshop and garden. The monks spent all day alone, meeting only for services in the church, and though their houses were quite comfortable, their food was sparse and entirely vegetarian.

Richard Methley, a monk of Mount Grace in the late fifteenth century, wrote an account of one of his mystical experiences:

> After celebrating Mass [I] was engaged upon thanksgiving in prayer and meditation, when God visited me in power, and I yearned with love so as almost to give up the ghost. Then did I forget all pain and fear and deliberate thought of any thing, and even of the Creator...first I oft commended

my soul to God, saying: 'Into thy hands', either in words or (as I think rather) in spirit. But as the pain of love grew more powerful I could scarce have any thought at all, forming within my spirit these words: 'Love! Love! Love!' And at last, ceasing from this, I deemed that I would wholly yield up my soul, singing, rather than crying, in spirit through joy: Ah! Ah! Ah!

This account, which finds echoes in the words of mystics of many traditions and ages, perfectly summarises the aim of Carthusian spirituality: the unique encounter between solitary and God, in the privacy of his sacred place.

MOW COP

One of the ways places become 'sacred' is by being the site of a key event in religious history. Mow Cop is a large rocky hill among the small farms, former coal mines, stone quarries and scruffy pit villages of Staffordshire, and is a place of great importance to many Methodist Christians because it was here that an outdoor revival meeting took place in 1807, that led to the founding of Primitive Methodism.

Camp Meetings were an American idea – great open-air rallies where preachers inspired the enthusiasm of the masses through rousing sermons and prayer. An earnest group of local Methodists were stirred with the idea of holding one at Mow Cop. This was mainly a meeting for prayer, but it attracted thousands of working-class people from the towns and villages. Prayers began at six in the morning, and as the rain stopped and the sun came out vast crowds began to arrive. They came from the local towns and villages from miles around: farm labourers, potters, silk-weavers, miners, and workers of all sorts, with a scattering of more well-to-do folk. There were six separate 'preaching stands'. Many of the

preachers described their own conversion. One told his story in verse: had been a shepherd boy, been press-ganged, shipwrecked, captured by French soldiers, and become an anti-slavery and temperance campaigner. An Irish lawyer told of the horrors of the Irish Rebellion in which he lost all his worldly goods, but was converted by an American evangelist. Another preacher was 'Peg-leg' Eleazer Hathorn, who told how he had been a Deist, and an army officer, how he had lost a leg in a war in Africa, but had been converted and now spoke of the 'happiness of our land and of the gratitude we owed to God for its exemption from being the seat of war.'

So successful was the day, and so much enthusiasm and spiritual fervour was generated, that a second, more organised, meeting was arranged for two months later.

One of the principal organisers of the meetings was the 35-year-old Hugh Bourne, a devout, shy and earnest mill-wright and joiner, son of a 'drunken and violent' farmer from Bucknall. His enthusiasm for open-air revivalism led to his expulsion from the Methodist Church – just as, fifty years earlier,

the Anglican Church had effectively expelled John Wesley. As a result, Bourne and the much more charismatic twenty-six-year-old William Clowes, a potter's son from Burslem, founded the Primitive Methodists.

Orthodox Methodism had become respectable, chapel-going, almost Middle Class. It had abandoned open-air preaching, and was only too conscious that public opinion linked dissent, radicalism and French revolutionary sympathies. By contrast the Primitive Methodists were rough, working-class and radical; Orthodox Methodism was a religion for the poor, Primitive Methodism was a religion of the poor.

During the following generation Primitive Methodism spread throughout the country. It was particularly strong in industrial areas, where it made a great contribution to the development of trade unions, and to radical politics generally: in 1832 six miners claiming to be Primitive Methodists were transported to Botany Bay for taking part in a strike at Jarrow. But it took a strong hold among the agricultural workers of Lincolnshire and East

Anglia, where the little brick chapels defied squire and parson and supported the Agricultural Workers Union. By mid-century Primitive Methodism was a well-organised church not only in the United Kingdom but in The United States, Australia, New Zealand and elsewhere.

above: The imitation ruin of Mow Cop Castle.

opposite: The rock formation known as 'The Old Man of Mow'.

ROSEDENE, GREAT DODFORD

And yet again the scene is changed,
'Location Day' arrives,
O'Connor's boys come settling here
Like bees from busy hives.
The gay procession wends its way,
The waggons and the gigs,
'Fergus and Freedom' flaunts aloft,
'Less parsons and more pigs'.

Just as there are many places dedicated to religious purposes, so there are places where people have tried to keep religion out. The anti-religious tradition in England is long and honourable, though it was often forced underground and its history is difficult to trace, particularly in earlier centuries.

Much easier to find than real atheism is opposition to the clergy and the church, which was often the target of radical criticism and attack. Even so, political radicalism was closely associated with free thinking, and opposition to the power of the Established Church often spilled over into opposition to religion itself. This was hardly surprising when their enemies called Chartists 'Republicans, Infidels, Sabbath-breakers and Blasphemers'. Chartism was a radical political movement that sought real democracy and social justice through the reform of Parliament. It reached its highest point in 1842 when a second Great Petition for 'The Peoples' Charter' was presented, with three million signatures.

A contemporary novel has a Chartist working man remark of religion in general: 'There was very little real enmity against it, as far as I could see, among working men. We only thought it a humbug, and not worth a sensible man troubling his head about'.

One of Chartism's leaders was the controversial and increasingly maverick Irishman, Feargus O'Connor. When Chartism failed to hold together as a political – let alone a revolutionary – movement, after the rejection of the third Great Petition, O'Connor turned to direct local action. He set up a company to purchase land and to give poor workers a cottage, a plot of land, and the vote. Though O'Connor was no manager and the company soon went bankrupt, five new smallholding estates were created, of which Great Dodford, near Bromsgrove, Worcestershire, was the last. It was split into forty plots, each having a substantial cottage, with well, dairy, pigsty and four acres of land.

The great 'location day', when the subscribers took up occupation, came on 2 July 1849; they included a carpenter, grocer, hatter, mason, pawnbroker and plumber, as well as farmers and gardeners. It was a former gardener who realised that with lots of manure the heavy red soil would serve for a market garden, and it was growing strawberries for the Birmingham market that was the saving of the estate. The first occupier of 'Rosedene' was William Hodgkiss, an East India Company pensioner from Cork.

Though the early settlers' independence earned the epithet 'rag, tag and bobtail' from one

local parson, a generation later a mission church and a Baptist Chapel were opened, and by 1900 any radical anti-clericalism seems to have largely faded away. The poem quoted above, which must surely incorporate family memories, was composed in 1900 for the opening of church rooms and the collection of funds for a new permanent church.

opposite top: The dairy at Rosedene.

opposite left: Hostility to religion comes out clearly in the songs of John Lennon, whose childhood home – 'Mendips, in Woolton, Liverpool – now belongs to the National Trust. In 'Working-class Hero' he attacks those who 'Keep you doped with religion and sex and TV', while 'Imagine' is almost an atheist anthem:

> Imagine there's no heaven,
> It's easy if you try,
> No hell below us,
> Above us only sky…

ST JOHN'S JERUSALEM

Sacred places have too often been the scene of intolerance and conflict, as different groups have tried to impose their different understandings both on their rivals and on the place itself.

The Holy Land, and especially Jerusalem, has always been a superlatively sacred place for Jews, Christians and Moslems alike. The followers of each of those religions have understood the city in their own terms, and whenever they could they have physically reconstructed it to suit their own understanding. But the Holy Land has been as important to all three religions as a memory and a symbol as it has been as a physical place, and it has been as contested in the minds of devotees as on the ground.

The Knights of the Hospital of St John of Jerusalem began as a small religious order dedicated to looking after the welfare of Christian pilgrims to Jerusalem. Too soon, however, they became involved in Holy Land politics, their role in protecting pilgrims led them to develop an army, and they became a major force in the crusades, flourishing under the crusader kingdom. Under Raymond of Provence (1120–60) they built a large hospital near the Holy Sepulchre, and as they steadily amassed huge wealth they changed from a purely charitable order to an order with three classes: the military brothers, the brothers infirmarians, and the brothers chaplains. After the fall of Jerusalem the Knights of St John fled from the Holy Land, but for the next three centuries the Order was a major player in world politics, and from its base on Rhodes played an important role in resisting Ottoman Turkish expansion.

Though people sometimes point to nobler motives and to heroic deeds, the fact is that the Order quickly became corrupted, and its hatred of Moslems – indeed all 'others' – was expressed in a shameful fanaticism and cruelty.

The Order's 'commanderies' in Europe, though they offered hospitality to travellers, were there principally to support its work in the Middle East, by forwarding money and recruits. At the height of their power in the Holy Land the Order possessed seven castles and 140 estates, while in Europe they were said to hold 19,000 manors. The lands attached to a single house were placed under the

command of a knight of the order, called preceptor or commander. He collected the revenues, part of which was devoted to the support of his community, and part sent to the houses of the Holy Land.

The commandery at Sutton-at-Hone in Kent probably only ever housed a handful of brothers; it was refounded in 1214, and survived some 150 years. There-after the site became a private estate; in the 18th century it was the home of Edward Hasted, the Kent historian, whose reference to a local lane seems to have begun the whole legend of the Pilgrim's Way from Winchester to Canterbury. Of the commandery today only the chapel, with its buttressed flint walls and three tall lancet windows, survives.

above: St John's Jerusalem.

opposite: Crac des Chevaliers ('Castle of the Knights') in Syria, built by the Hospitallers in the early 1100s.

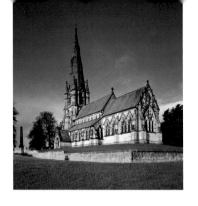

ST MARY'S, STUDLEY ROYAL

The best Victorian churches must be among the greatest of Britain's architectural legacy. They attracted the most imaginative architects and designers, and some of the wealthiest spenders. They also attracted huge enthusiasm, for they represented a new – or renewed – understanding of God and his Church, and their relationship to society.

The Gothic Revival was on one level just a style fashion: windows with pointed arches rather than round, columns modelled on medieval precedents, not Greek or Roman. For many of its protagonists, however, building in the Gothic style was a moral crusade, declaring a belief that the Church was created by God with a mission to include the whole world; that at the heart of the Church's work lay the Eucharist or Mass; and that the church building in which the Eucharist was celebrated was thereby a holy place whose design must express the glory of God, continuity with the 'Ages of Faith', and a particular understanding of society.

The Gothic Revival was closely linked to the Oxford Movement, which began as a protest by young dons at Oxford (the 'Tractarians') against government interference with the Church of England, and grew into a campaign to restore a Catholic understanding of the church. Like the High Church movement of the seventeenth century (*see* p.94), this one soon expressed itself in an emphasis on the beauty of worship, based more-or-less accurately on medieval practice. For the High Church wing of the Church of England, the Church was an autonomous, God-given institution, whose role was one of mission. It was natural, therefore, that the succeeding generations of Tractarians appealed, in their style as in their theology, to the medieval church they saw as supremely successfully independent.

A new plan for churches was adapted from the larger medieval church, which clearly set out the new understanding. From the people's nave – where everyone sat on similar benches, surrounded on the walls by tablets commemorating the dead – you moved up into the chancel, domain of the clergy and choir. Beyond was the most holy part of the church, the sanctuary surrounding the altar.

St Mary's Church at Studley Royal, North Yorkshire, built by the great William Burges and paid for by the 1st Marquis of Ripon, expresses this model in dramatic fashion. By the 1870s the Gothic style was almost universally accepted as the proper style for churches (though chapels often deliberately avoided it) and architects were becoming increasingly adventurous in using it. The lavish decoration and elaborate symbolism of the chancel is deliberately designed to declare that this is a sacred place. Separated from the nave where the people sat, the chancel is the place of the robed choir and clergy, while the sanctuary is the place of the altar. The walls are lined with alabaster, the shafts are coloured marble. In the floor are the principal buildings of Jerusalem, and the sanctuary pavement represents the Garden of Eden surrounded by the four rivers: Gihon, Pison, Tigris and Euphrates. Above, banks of painted angels support a gilded dome.

The National Trust has at least two other splendid Gothic Revival chapels. St Mary the Virgin, Clumber Park, Nottinghamshire, was designed ten years later than Studley Royal, for another aristocratic landowner, by the very

this page: St Mary's, Studley Royal: details of altar, ceiling and gilded angel.

opposite: Exterior view of St Mary's.

St Mary the Virgin,
Clumber Park,
Nottinghamshire.

different but equally great architect George Frederick Bodley. Here the altar is even more dominant, and the chancel separated from the nave by a medieval-style screen.

Besides aristocratic patrons, the Gothic Revival in England was greatly advanced by Victorian millionaires, who expressed their faith through it. William Gibbs was a deeply religious business-man who made a fortune importing guano for fertiliser, and who built, restored or contributed to over nineteen churches, as well as a large number of almshouses, schools, institutions and hospitals. In 1873 he added a sumptuous private chapel to his home, Tyntesfield House near Bristol, intending it to be his mausoleum. Designed by Arthur Blomfield, it was based (rather remotely) on Saint Louis' spectacular thirteenth-century chapel, the Sainte-Chapelle in Paris. It included mosaics by Salviati, stained glass by Powell, rich carving and metalwork. Gibbs's friend and relative, the novelist Charlotte Yonge, recalled: 'The erection of this beautiful chapel, with choral services daily and weekly cel-ebrations, gave a character to the household almost resembling that of Little Gidding'. It expressed in dramatic form the ideals of the Oxford Movement.

The mosaic reads: SAVL·WHY·PERSECVTEST·THOV·ME · SAINT·PAVL · NOTHING·SHALL·HVRT·YOV

above: The mosaic triptych behind the altar at Tyntesfield Chapel. Made by the celebrated glass firm, Salviati, it depicts scenes from the life of St Paul.

left: The chancel, Tyntesfield Chapel.

ST MICHAEL'S MOUNT

Mount Kilimanjaro in Africa, Mount Fuji in Japan, Mount Zion in Israel, Nandi Devi in India – holy mountains are found in most religious traditions. In England and Wales, as in France, this tradition is mainly represented by the hills dedicated to St Michael, of which St Michael's Mount in Cornwall is perhaps the best known.

The Revelation of St John describes how St Michael the Archangel led his angels in the heavenly war against the seven-headed dragon. Perhaps for that reason he became associated with hilltops.

Accessible along a causeway only at low tide, St Michael's Mount has attracted all sorts of legends. According to one, the Mount was built by the giant, Cormoran. Cormoran would wade ashore from the island to snatch cattle and sheep from the fields around Marazion. A farmer's son, Jack from Land's End, rowed out to the island during the night and dug a deep pit halfway up the northern slope of the Mount. In the morning Jack blew his horn: the giant awoke and ran down the hillside, but with the glare of the early morning sun dazzling his eyes he fell headlong into the pit. The grateful locals gave Jack the title 'Jack the Giant Killer'.

For most of the Middle Ages the Mount was occupied by a Benedictine priory, a daughter house of the Abbey of Mont St Michel in Normandy. It seems to have been a minor pilgrimage centre: during the Wars of the Roses some leading Lancastrians, fleeing from the Yorkists, got in disguised as pilgrims, and then held it against all comers. Fourteen years after the priory was closed in 1535, the Mount was the scene of the Prayer Book Rebellion. When the Governor of the Mount, Humphrey Arundell, was away, local protestors against the new English Prayer Book took possession. For the past three centuries, however, the Mount has been the agreeable home of the St Aubyn family.

SANDHAM MEMORIAL CHAPEL

It is an ancient human instinct to focus memory in a place; monuments as well as tombs have served as a way of reminding people of individual or collective experience, and of helping them to manage their memories. The National Trust has many examples of monuments and memorials, but few more dramatic and powerful than Sandham Memorial Chapel at Burghclere in Hampshire, with its famous Stanley Spencer murals.

The national and personal trauma of the First World War brought an intensified desire to create new shrines into which memories could be focussed, and new rituals to help focus them. The Remembrance Day ceremony at the Cenotaph in Whitehall, London, is still reflected in towns and villages throughout the country. Individuals also created their own shrines, if only a few photographs and mementos on a bedroom mantelpiece.

The Sandham Memorial Chapel was a memorial to a young lieutenant who died of an illness contracted in Macedonia. His sister and her husband, Mary and John Louis Behrend, were art collectors who already owned paintings by Stanley Spencer, and

they offered to build a chapel to display a series of paintings of war in Macedonia, where the artist had also spent two years fighting.

Stanley Spencer was one of the artists of the twentieth century with the strongest sense of place and of the spirituality inherent in place. He produced many paintings in which the Thameside village of Cookham where he lived was depicted as the Heavenly Jerusalem – but he also saw the spirituality in a requisitioned asylum in Bristol or in a dull bit of Macedonia:

> In the train I think from Lembet, to which we were, after a few days, marched, I sat on the wooden seats, and was entranced by the landscapes from the window, low plains with trees and looking through them to strange further plains or fields, and here and there a figure in dirty white. It was not a landscape; it was a spiritual world.

Stanley Spencer had served as a private in the army throughout the First World War, first scrubbing floors and carrying stretchers in a Bristol army hospital, then for two

years in northern Greece, with a field ambulance unit and later as an infantryman fighting the Bulgarians.

Sandham Memorial Chapel was consciously modelled on Giotto's 1305 Arena Chapel at Padua, which itself was a monument to his patron Enrico Scrovegni's father. Spencer's paintings, however, depicted not the life of Christ, but the most mundane and everyday life of common soldiers in wartime. Yet he transformed them onto a spiritual plane, a transfiguration that becomes explicit on the east wall, where the resurrected soldiers pile up their crosses above the altar and before Christ.

Details of the Stanley
Spencer paintings at
Sandham Memorial Chapel.
opposite: *Reveille.*
above: *Resurrection*, from
above the altar.

right: Silver Birch trees in the chancel of Whipsnade Tree Cathedral, Bedfordshire. This was created in 1931 by E.K. Blyth who, inspired by the building of Liverpool Cathedral, wanted to commemorate his friends – Arthur Bailey, John Bennett and Francis Holland – killed in 1918 in the First World War. It is a collection of trees planted in the plan of a full-sized cathedral, with nave, transepts, chapels and cloister garden. The Tree Cathedral is an enclosure for meditation, worship of God and the peaceful enjoyment of nature.

opposite: Memorial room to Adrian Drewe at Castle Drogo, Devon, arranged by his mother after his death in Flanders in 1917.

SHAROW CROSS

This stump is the only survivor of the eight crosses that once marked the boundaries of the 'sanctuary' of St Wilfrid's monastery in Ripon, North Yorkshire. In very many cultures there have been particular places – cities, villages, houses or spots – where it is forbidden to harm another person, and where a fugitive from justice or from an enemy can find asylum. Often these are sacred places, and the fugitive puts him or herself under the protection of the local deity or saint, whose home the sanctuary is. In ancient Greece, and later in Rome, many sanctuaries offered asylum, and the deity was said to punish violators severely. It seems quite likely that pagan Saxon sanctuaries were inviolate in this sense, for *fri geard*, 'sanctuary', comes from the combining of the Old English words for 'to protect' and 'yard'.

Churches claimed the same privileges, and in medieval England the fugitive only had to reach a church or other religious building to claim sanctuary for forty days. Twelfth-century law declared that anyone laying violent hands on a fugitive in a cathedral or abbey was subject to a fine of a hundred shillings, but a parish church merited only twenty shillings and a chapel a mere ten.

When the forty days were up, the fugitive had three choices. He could escape again, and perhaps become an outlaw. He could surrender to the Coroner or Sheriff – but that almost certainly meant hanging. Or he could decide to 'abjure the realm', meaning he could avoid trial and execution by leaving the country under a set routine prescribed by the Coroner.

Some monasteries provided more extensive, and even permanent, sanctuary, and as a result housed considerable numbers. At Beaulieu Abbey in Hampshire for instance, just before it was suppressed:

We find there are here sanctuary men for debt, felony and murder, thirty-two of them, many aged, some very sick; they have all of them wives and children and dwelling-houses and ground whereby they live. They have lamentably declared that if they are sent away, they shall be utterly undone. We have certain knowledge that the greater numbers of them should be utterly cast away, their age and impotence and other things considered.

Ripon's right to offer sanctuary was given by King Alfred's grandson, King Athelstan, when he added Yorkshire to his kingdom. Fugitives could flee to Ripon and live there under the protection of St Wilfrid for a specified time. The area within which they were protected extended one mile from the church in every direction, and there was a scale of fines for molesting refugees: between the limit and the graveyard £18; within the graveyard £36; within the choir, confiscation of goods and possible death.

Those who sought sanctuary were called 'grythmen' and were under the spiritual charge of a 'gryth-priest'. They were under the protection of St Wilfrid, just as a fugitive in a Greek temple was under the protection of Apollo, or indeed a guest under the protection of his or her host. Both had duties: at Ripon the grythmen undertook, among other things, to carry the banners before the relics of St Wilfrid in certain processions.

STAUNTON HAROLD

In the yeare: 1653
When all things sacred were throughout ye nation
Either demolishd or profaned
Sr Robert Shirley Baronet
Founded this church
Whose singular praise it is
To have done the best things in the worst times
And
Hoped them in the most callamitous
The Righteous shall be had in everlasting remembrance

Sir Robert Shirley was powerful enough to defy Cromwell's government by creating a church which, in all its arrangements, art and decoration, symbolised the belief that this was a sacred place. He was a Royalist and an old-fashioned High Anglican in a revolutionary world where his enemies held power, and he wanted to declare to the world his beliefs and his optimism. Over the door of his new church he placed his provocative inscription.

From the beginning Christians have disputed to what extent physical things can be imbued with, or can represent, the holy. The dispute was at its fiercest in England in the middle of the seventeenth century. For Roman Catholics and High Anglicans, objects as well as people could be consecrated, because of their dedication to God's service. For Puritans, consecrated people alone were God's true temples.

The Civil War had many causes, and people who fought in it had many motives. For very many protagonists, however, the kind of ceremonies performed in church – and the church's furnishings and decoration – were central, for they reflected an understanding of the church, of God, and of society itself.

Those Royalists who looked back to the policy of Archbishop Laud believed that there was an intimate connection between 'the outward sense of God' and the inward. Moreover, an emphasis on ceremony, symbolism and beauty went with a belief in uniformity and discipline, and in a church and a society obedient to its bishops and to its divinely-ordained king.

For these High Anglicans, the ultimate symbol was the altar, protected by railings and raised up on steps at the east end of the church. Laud had called it 'the greatest place of God's residence upon earth'. It symbolised the 'Eucharistic Sacrifice' and hierarchy, just as a communion table in the middle of the chancel symbolised the 'Lord's Supper' and democracy.

Few would have gone as far as to say (as some continental Catholics did) that the church building was inherently sacred, but it was rendered holy by its dedication and its use for holy purposes. Staunton Harold in Leicestershire is one of the very few churches built during Cromwell's rule, and in every part it declares that 'this is a sacred place'. Through the door the worshipper passes under an organ loft into the nave, where above the panelled walls, box pews, minister's pew and pulpit, the ceiling is now painted with the theme of Creation out of Chaos, all clouds and rays of light.

In the spacious chancel the

worshippers came and kneeled for Communion, originally at movable kneeling forms, permanently covered with dark purple houseling cloths. The altar, a solid oak table, stands on three steps and is covered with a carpet of rich velvet with a gold fringe and embroidered symbols: the letters IHS (Jesus), a cross, sacred heart, and a glory issuing from the crown of thorns. Originally there stood on the altar two prayer books engraved with the crucifix, and two candlesticks. In use the altar was completely covered with a fair linen cloth, and bore the silver-gilt communion plate. On the ceiling above is the word 'Theos', surrounded with cherubim's heads, which are represented as singing alternately, 'Hallelujah' and 'Sanctus, Sanctus, Sanctus'.

The historians Addleshaw and Etchells comment that John Inglesant, hero of a novel of the period, might have been thinking of just such a church when he said that 'upon the altars of our Church "the divine presence hovers as surely to those who believe it, as it does upon the splendid altars of Rome"'.

right: Inscription over the west door.

SUTTON HOO

Eminent people have throughout history used elaborate funerals and monuments to demonstrate their power. On a high promontory over the river Deben in southeast Suffolk, very probably close to the site of the royal court, stand the burial mounds of some of the earliest kings of East Anglia.

Around 600, some of the Anglo-Saxon aristocrats of England were beginning to aspire to be kings. The old society of the lord and his retainers feasting between raids in their hall was giving way to the idea of the kingdom, where one lord was superior and could maintain his position less by war than by taxation. This was also the time when Christian missionaries were aggressively promoting their faith, and in many parts of England the powerful were looking to Gaul for their example, and copying its Christianity, its kingdoms, and its Roman culture. This is the world the Venerable Bede – writing in around 730 – describes so vividly.

A few would-be kings, however, looked for their example not to Gaul but to pagan Scandinavia, and sought to remain true to their own pagan past. Among these were the first kings of East Anglia.

Bede describes how Rædwald, one of the strongest of them, did flirt with Christianity, but his wife soon persuaded him out of it. By way of compromise, he set up a Christian altar alongside the others in his temple.

Little is known about East Ang-lian paganism in this period, how it may have differed from paganism elsewhere in Britain or Europe, or what it meant to people in practice. Temples seem to have contained many images and altars, served by a priesthood. The celestial region of Asgard included

many gods: notably Woden, god of war, runes and poetry; Thor, god of thunder and the sky; and Tiw – all of whose names survive in days of the week. There were many lesser deities with their own seasons and holy days.

The secrets of the burial mounds at Sutton Hoo lay undiscovered until the first modern excavation in 1939 uncovered the impression of a huge ship and a collection of precious objects which had, amazingly, managed to escape the looters. This was the richest of the Sutton Hoo barrows, and it seems most likely that the man buried in it is Rædwald, and that burial in a ship was a deliberate imitation of Scandinavian practice, a very public display of pagan ideology. Buried with him were his personal items (rich clothes, a jewelled purse and

ornaments); his weapons (a helmet and shield, a jewelled sword and spears); symbols of his kingship (a whetstone sceptre and an iron standard), and symbols of hospitality (a lyre in its beaverskin bag, Byzantine silver bowls, bone gaming pieces, cauldrons, horns and drinking cups). All were of extraordinary quality and can be seen today in the British Museum.

Such an elaborate burial implies an equally elaborate funeral. The famous poem *Beowulf* ends with the hero's funeral: 'Upon the headland the Geats erected a broad, high tumulus, plainly visible to distant seamen. In ten days they completed the building of the hero's beacon...Within the barrow they placed collars, brooches, and all the trappings which they had plundered from the treasure-hoard...Then twelve chieftains, all sons of princes, rode round the barrow lamenting their loss, speaking of their king, reciting an elegy, and acclaiming the hero...So the Geats who had shared his hall mourned the death of their lord...'. Perhaps the Wuffings, the family of Rædwald, did the same.

As the cemetery's most recent excavator puts it:

The Anglo-Saxon cemetery at Sutton Hoo can be seen as a short-lived and extravagant ceremonial centre of the late sixth and early seventh century CE, the purpose of which was to provide a focus for a policy of pagan independence...The investment in an overtly pagan style of burial at Sutton Hoo may have been directly provoked by the perceived menace of a predatory Christian mission.

To visitors arriving from the river, the great burial mounds said 'this is our land – we are pagan and proud of it'.

left: Replica of ceremonial helmet found at Sutton Hoo.

right: Contemporary photograph of the latter stage of the 1939 excavation of mound 1, revealing the form of the buried ship.

SUTTON HOUSE

The idea of ghosts having anything to do with sacred places may seem absurd. Yet ghosts notoriously cling to particular places and the haunted house is therefore very much a 'special place'. Haunted places, like many sacred places, are where the relationship of the living and the dead is somehow managed.

A number of theories have been put forward in an attempt to explain ghosts, but the one which perhaps links most closely to a sense of place is the idea that a past event can be imprinted on the surroundings by the powerful emotional energy it once generated. This is then 'seen', almost like a photograph, and is sometimes referred to as a 'place memory'.

Many believe that the dead can reveal themselves to the living, and while ghosts appear in very many cultures, the form they take and the explanations given for them depend on prevalent beliefs at particular times and can vary according to locality. In medieval Yorkshire, for example, it was thought that tormented souls manifesting themselves in terrifying shapes found peace when they were posthumously absolved of

their sins. After the Reformation, some thought ghosts were devils in disguise, whilst others thought the dead were returning either to help and advise the living, or to seek for themselves some kind of reassurance.

Interest in ghosts increased enormously in the later nineteenth century, along with a multitude of other manifestations of 'the other world', including thought-reading, clairvoyance, telepathy, mesmeric trance, automatic writing, apparitions, and the like; it is perhaps no coincidence that this fashion coincided with the decline among the middle classes of more traditional and formal religious belief. Indeed, the arrival of spiritualism from the US in the 1850s, and the founding of spiritualist churches, added a more formal dimension to the belief that mediumship (in which a living person becomes the channel for communication with the dead) can prove that the human spirit survives physical death.

The National Trust has innumerable properties to which ghost stories have become attached. Sutton House, a Tudor building in the centre of Hackney in East London, is just one

example. Here there have been many reported sightings of a figure in long white clothes, believed to be the ghost of Frances Machell, who died in childbirth there in 1574. In the late 1980s a photograph was taken at a private party in the café bar, and when the film was developed, a white figure with outstretched arms could be seen standing in the foreground. On other occasions, staff have reported sudden drops in temperature, the doors of cabinets opening of their own accord and objects like candles and noticeboards flying across rooms unaided. The barking of dogs and the voices of tiny children have been heard when the house has been closed to the public, but live dogs refuse to enter certain parts of the house. During a recent refurbishment, someone sleeping on the premises was woken by a 'blue woman' shaking the bed. A séance was subsequently held at the house by local spiritualists, who claimed that there were many spirits in residence – most of them benevolent, except for two known as 'Tim' and 'George', between whom there appeared to be a great deal of bad feeling. By coincidence a local historian had

been examining public records relating to the house, and only a few days before the séance (but before he had had time to tell anyone of his findings) he had discovered that in 1752 Sutton House was divided into two parts.

One half was rented to a Timothy Ravenhill, and the other to a George Garrett ... no evidence has yet been found of any enmity between these two, but research continues.

above: The Armada Window at Sutton House.

opposite: The Linenfold Chamber.

Ham House

The stately homes of England,
though rather in the lurch
Provide a lot of chances for
psychical research

One of the stateliest of the homes
Noel Coward sang of is Ham
House, situated in one of the
greener parts of West London. It
has indeed been the object of
much psychical research, for it is
splendidly haunted. The principal
ghost is said to be the beautiful
Elizabeth Murray, who inherited
the house in 1655 and was
described as '...restless in her
ambition, profuse in her expense,
and of a most ravenous covet-
ousness'. Her rapid re-marriage
after the convenient death of her
first husband gave her a dubious
reputation, but also the title of
Duchess of Lauderdale, and the
funds to rebuild Ham House in the
height of fashion.

She is regularly seen about the
house, and so sometimes are the
Duke, his chaplain and her dog.
Other regular hauntings include
the scream of a suicide, smells of
roses and tobacco, moving
furniture, noises of all sorts, and
occasionally tour guides being
pushed downstairs by a mysterious
hand.

A recent night-time investig-
ation by the Ghost Club not only
identified the rose smell very
strongly, but conducted a
'conversation' – by means of
dowsing rods – with the young
Elizabeth Murray, the Duke's
chaplain and an eighteenth-
century chambermaid called Jenny
(who died of poison). They also
photographed strange orbs of
light.

right: Places are often said to have an 'atmosphere', and houses to retain the 'presence' of their occupants. One visitor to T.E. Lawrence's ('Lawrence of Arabia') Dorset cottage remarked that 'I have never had such a strong impression that the owner of a house was still present, after death, as I have in Lawrence's'.

left: The main staircase at Ham House.

below: The Cherry Garden at Ham House, with statue of the god Bacchus.

TATTON PARK

The ancient religion of Japan – Shinto, 'the way of the gods' – saw all of nature as inhabited by the gods, but some mountains, rocky cliffs, caves, springs, trees and stones were their particular home. Shinto priests carried out ceremonies there to ask for the gods' protection. After the sixth century Buddhism began to make inroads into Japan, and the art of garden-making was imported, along with other Buddhist cultural forms, from Korea and China. The ancient Shinto tradition was easily incorporated into the new approach, since Buddhism also valued particular natural forms – such as stones, water or hills – for their inherent power as well as for their beauty.

From the beginning, Japanese gardens were designed with a view to creating both a place of spiritual power and a picture to gaze on and walk through. Japanese Buddhism suggested the image of paradise: the 'Pure Land' of heaven presided over by Amida Buddha. The Pure Land could be represented in more detail as an island; a pond could represent the vast ocean that separates profane mortals from heaven; a bridge could represent the possibility of universally attainable salvation.

This understanding of landscape was based on the opposing yet complementary principles of Yin (the negative, passive force) and Yang (the positive, active force) and their mutual effects on the five basic elements: wood, fire, earth, gold (metal), and water. Early Japanese gardeners used these principles to design the flow of water, and to position specific plants or rocks, believed to be imbued with particular properties, in order to create a harmonic state within the garden.

Over the centuries the Japanese evolved a number of styles of garden. Those of the early aristocrats were deeply poetic, consciously designed to offer the same images as contemporary nature poems. In the medieval period a new form of garden developed in Zen Buddhist temples and warriors' houses, in which a small and very simple garden was created as an object of contemplation and aid to meditation. These Zen gardens were created of just evergreen plants, rocks, and sand or moss. The development of the tea ceremony brought about a third form of garden, one through which one walks, letting go the cares of the world as one approaches the teahouse. The calm enjoyment of this simple ritual assisted participants in attaining unity with their surroundings and the universe.

The Japanese garden at Tatton Park, Cheshire, brings together elements of many different styles. It includes a tea house, a Shinto shrine brought from Japan, a representation of Mount Fuji and a *kasatei* or rest house. It contains many Japanese plants, such as maples, azaleas, cherry and ferns. The ground has a mantle of moss, creating the atmosphere of a *saihouji* or moss temple. The garden was constructed between 1910 and 1913 by Japanese craftsmen for the owner Alan de Tatton Egerton, who had just visited the Japan Exhibition in London.

It has recently been restored under the supervision of Professor Masao Fukuhara, a well-known garden designer and historian based at Osaka University. The Tatton Park garden is considered by many to be one of the finest examples in Europe, for it went much further than most in capturing the philosophy that created the true Japanese garden.

TŶ MAWR WYBRNANT

Throughout Welsh history there seems to have been a tradition that saw the whole of Wales as a 'holy land'. The prophets, preachers and hymn-writers who carried this tradition often identified the people of Wales with the people of Israel, and the idea of the Welsh as a chosen people was greatly strengthened by their universal familiarity, for three and more centuries, with the Welsh Bible. Here the land, its people, their language and the Book come together.

Tŷ Mawr Wybrnant is a small stone-built house in the heart of Snowdonia, once the home of William Morgan, translator of the Bible into Welsh. William Morgan, the Rector of Llanrhaeadr-ym-Mochnant, spent ten years translating the Old Testament and revising the earlier translation of the New Testament. A scholar in Hebrew and Greek, he was summoned to Lambeth and his abilities vetted by the Archbishop of Canterbury, John Whitgift, who then made him his chaplain, encouraged him to complete his translation, and paid for its printing. In 1588, the year of the Spanish Armada, 800 copies of the Welsh Bible were printed.

Queen Elizabeth I's government was working to incorporate Wales into England, and to bring all Welsh people into the Church of England. But beyond Offa's Dyke, church services in English were even less accessible to monoglot Welshmen than the colourful old Latin mass they had replaced. Morgan's translation meant that every church in Wales could now at least have a copy of the Bible in the language of the people.

Like Luther's German translation and the King James Version in England, Morgan's Welsh Bible shaped the nation, keeping the Welsh language alive when it might so easily have declined into a variety of local dialects, or even died out. Instead, it became the foundation and inspiration of Welsh as a written language. The classical language of Morgan's Bible has left an indelible imprint upon Welsh thought and culture.

UFFINGTON WHITE HORSE

Despite legends that the White Horse at Uffington, Berkshire, was constructed by King Alfred to commemorate his victory over the Danes in 871, or by Hengist, the leader of the Anglo-Saxon horde in the fifth century CE, archaeologists have recently shown that it is actually some 3,000 years old, and dates from the early Bronze Age, a time when this part of Berkshire was becoming increasingly populous. Perhaps it was a tribal symbol, depicting the sacred animal in order to mark out territory. Local folklore maintained that it is in fact a dragon, marking out the site on Dragon Hill immediately below, where legend has it that St George fought and killed the mythical beast.

Whatever its original purpose, it has been used in all sorts of ways over the centuries. Throughout the eighteenth century, and up until 1857, the 'scouring' of the White Horse by the villagers of Uffington every few years was always accompanied by a lively country fair; in 1780, some 30,000 people were there on Whit Monday. In 1776 a leaflet announced:

> The scowering and cleansing of the White Horse is fixed for Monday the 27th day of May; on which day a Silver Cup will be run for near White Horse Hill, by any horse &c. that never run for anything, carrying 11 stone, the best of 3 two-mile heats, to start at ten o'clock. Between the heats will be run for by Poneys, a Saddle, Bridle and Whip; the best of 3 two-mile heats, the winner of 2 heats will be entitled to the Saddle, the second best the Bridle, and the third the Whip.
> The same time a Thill harness will be run for by Cart-horses, &c. in their harness and bells, the carters to ride in smock frocks without saddles, crossing and jostling, but no whipping allowed.
> A flitch of Bacon to be run for by asses.
> A good Hat to be run for by men in sacks, every man to bring his own sack.
> A Waistcoat, 10s. 6d. value, to be given to the person who shall take a bullet out of a tub of flour with his mouth in the shortest time.
> A Cheese to be run for down the White Horse Manger.
> Smocks to be run for by ladies, the second best of each prize to be entitled to a Silk Hat.

opposite: *The Vale of the White Horse* by Eric Ravilious (1903–42), c. 1939.

More than just fun, such celebrations are said by some historians to have been important means of preserving customary economic rights to land. The scouring fair, with its traditional rituals and traditional site, reinforced by ancient legends, claimed Uffington people's right of access to the downs. In Victorian times these popular festivals were either suppressed, or taken over by the respectable classes, cleaned up (no more drunkenness and riot) and given a new role in recalling that Merrie England that was becoming so important to the middle-class psyche. Some historians see this as marking a fundamental change in English society, from one where people were ruled by ancient mutual obligations, to one where all activities were like commodities, bought and sold.

The Cerne Giant

The Cerne Giant, or 'the Rude Man', as he has been called, is another site which has both attracted many legends and has been used by local people for community festivals and activities.

Who he is remains the subject of vigorous debate. Does he date from around the time of the Roman invasion? The club that he carries suggests he could be a representation of Hercules, which has led to speculation that this links him to the Emperor Commodus (180–193CE), who believed himself a reincarnation of the god. Alternatively, was he created by medieval monks from the nearby abbey as a mocking joke against their notorious abbot, Thomas Corton? Or was he created in the seventeenth century by the local landowner Denzil Holles, whose lands were seized after the Civil War, as a caricature of Oliver Cromwell? Modern opinion mainly inclines to the last theory, though proof is elusive. Tellingly, there is no mention of him in medieval records; the first reference dates back to a churchwarden's register from 1694, noting a payment of three shillings for maintenance work on the figure.

However ancient he may be, and whatever the reason he was created, the Giant has been used for all sorts of purposes and has for many come to represent a very special place. Local legend – which offers another explanation for his origins, that he marks the outline of the body of a giant slain on the hill – has attached mysterious powers to him. Sleeping on the body of the giant was said to ensure pregnancy, and in the 1920s this legend was sufficiently widely known to attract visitors from much further afield than Dorset. Young women wanting to ensure fidelity in their lovers were apparently encouraged to walk around him three times.

The site was also the focus of communal festivities. An ancient earthwork adjacent to the Giant known as the 'Frying Pan' or 'Trendle' was used as the site for dancing, which lasted until the late nineteenth century. Cerne's sexton remembered that in mid-Victorian times a maypole:

> ...was made every year from a fir-bole, and was raised in the night. It was erected in the ring just above the Giant. It was decorated, and the villagers went up the hill and danced round the pole on the 1st of May.

GAZETTEER

Details of National Trust properties, including opening times and how to get there, can be found on the Trust's extensive website: www.nationaltrust.org.uk.

Information about smaller, unstaffed, sites can be obtained from the relevant Regional Office.

Avebury
Marlborough
Wiltshire
SN8 1RF
01672 539250
avebury@nationaltrust.org.uk

Borrowdale
The National Trust
North West Regional Office
The Hollens
Grasmere
Ambleside
Cumbria
LA22 9QZ
0870 609 5391

Chedworth Roman Villa
Yanworth
Cheltenham
Gloucestershire
GL54 3LJ
01242 890256
chedworth@nationaltrust.org.uk

Clandon Park
West Clandon
Guildford
Surrey
GU4 7RQ
01483 222482
clandonpark@nationaltrust.org.uk

Farne Islands
The Farne Islands Property Manager
The Sheiling
8 St Aidans
Seahouses
Northumberland
NE68 7SR
01665 720651

Giant's Causeway
44a Causeway Road
Bushmills
Co. Antrim
BT57 8SU
028 2073 1582
giantscauseway@nationaltrust.org.uk

Glastonbury Tor
The National Trust
Wessex Regional Office
Eastleigh Court
Bishopstrow
Warminster
Wiltshire
BA12 9HW
01985 843600

Greys Court
Rotherfield Greys
Henley-on-Thames
Oxfordshire
RG9 4PG
01491 628529
greyscourt@nationaltrust.org.uk

Hailes Abbey
Winchcombe
Cheltenham
Gloucestershire
GL54 5PB
01242 602398
customers@english-heritage.org.uk

Holystone
The National Trust
Yorkshire & North East Regional Office
Goddards
27 Tadcaster Road
YORK
YO24 1GG
01904 702021

Housesteads Fort
Bardon Mill
Hexham
Northumberland
NE47 6NN
01434 344363

Kedleston Hall
Derby
Derbyshire
DE22 5JH
01332 843404
kedlestonhall@nationaltrust.org.uk

The Lake District
The National Trust
North West Regional Office
The Hollens
Grasmere
Ambleside
Cumbria
LA22 9QZ
0870 609 5391

Lavenham Guildhall
Market Place
Lavenham
Sudbury
Suffolk
CO10 9QZ
01787 247646
lavenhamguildhall@nationaltrust.org.uk

Loughwood Meeting House
The National Trust
Devon & Cornwall Regional Office
Killerton House
Broadclyst
Exeter
EX5 3LE
01392 881691

Mount Grace Priory
Osmotherley
Northallerton
North Yorkshire
DL6 3JG
01609 883494

Mow Cop
The National Trust
West Midlands Regional Office
Clumber Park Stableyard
Worksop
Nottinghamshire
S80 3BE
01909 486411

Rosedene, Great Dodford
The National Trust
West Midlands Regional Office
Clumber Park Stableyard
Worksop
Nottinghamshire
S80 3BE
01909 486411

St John's Jerusalem
The National Trust
South East Regional Office
Polesden Lacey
Dorking
Surrey
RH5 6BD
01372 453401

St Mary's, Studley Royal
Fountains
Ripon
North Yorkshire
HG4 3DY
01765 608888

St Michael's Mount
Marazion
Penzance
Cornwall
TR17 0EF
01736 710265
godolphin@manor-office.co.uk

Sandham Memorial Chapel
Harts Lane
Burghclere
Newbury
Hampshire
RG20 9JT
01635 278394
sandham@nationaltrust.org.uk

Sharow Cross
The National Trust
Yorkshire & North East Regional Office
Goddards
27 Tadcaster Road
York
YO24 1GG
01904 702021

Staunton Harold Church
Staunton Harold
Ashby-de-la-Zouch
Leicestershire
01332 863822 (Calke Abbey)
stauntonharold@nationaltrust.org.uk

Sutton Hoo
Woodbridge
Suffolk
IP12 3DJ
01394 389700

Sutton House
2 & 4 Homerton High Street
Hackney
London E6 6JQ
020 8986 2264
suttonhouse@nationaltrust.org.uk

Tatton Park
Knutsford
Cheshire
WA16 6QN
01625 534400
tatton@cheshire.gov.uk

Tŷ Mawr Wybrnant
Penmachno
Bettws-y-Coed
Conwy
LL25 0HJ
01960 760213

Uffington White Horse
The National Trust
South East Regional Office
Polesden Lacey
Dorking
Surrey
RH5 6BD
01372 453401

OTHER SACRED PLACES

The National Trust cares for a great many other places, some of them quite unusual, which illustrate the themes discussed in this book. A few more examples are noted here.

Prehistoric Ceremonial Landscape

Kettle Lake, on the southern edge of Belfast, Northern Ireland, has been suspected of being part of a Bronze Age ritual landscape, perhaps for ritual deposit and sacrifice.

The Sacred Yew

The Ankerwycke Priory yew is one of the most ancient. It stands on the opposite bank of the Thames to Runnymede, where Magna Carta was signed, and it was then already fully grown. The yews at Fountains Abbey in Yorkshire were there when Cistercian monks first arrived in 1135.

Nature and Celtic Spirituality

St Herbert's Island on Derwentwater, Cumbria, was the home of a close friend of St Cuthbert, whom he visited at Lindisfarne every year. They died on the same day in 687. Herbert was largely forgotten for centuries after that, but in the fourteenth century the island became a place of pilgrimage.

Myth and Landscape

Ancient myths attach to many National Trust properties. Just one other example is Dunseverick Castle, a few miles along the coast from the Giant's Causeway, where Deirdre of the Sorrows landed on her return from exile in Scotland 2,000 years ago. Conal Cearnach, leader of the Red Branch Knights, lived there; he is said to have witnessed the crucifixion. In the fifth century St Patrick consecrated Olcan, the first Irish bishop, there, and from Dunseverick Fergus the Great and his brothers sailed to western Scotland in the 6th century, to found a kingdom and give the name 'Scotland' to Alba.

Pilgrimage

The Clive Museum at Powis Castle in Wales exhibits figures of Vishnu and other Hindu deities, which reflect the tradition of the great pilgrimage temples of South India.

Holy Wells

Of St Non's Well near St David's, Pembrokeshire, it was said in 1717 that: 'People go still to visit this Saint at some particular Times, especially upon St Nun's Day (2 March) which they keep holy, and offer Pins, Pebbles, Etc, at this well'. St Non was the mother of St David, and her well was said to cure all kinds of complaints; children were regularly dipped, even in the eighteenth century. In 1951 both the well and the nearby chapel were restored and re-dedicated.

St Bertram's Well at Ilam in Derbyshire commemorates an eighth-century Mercian prince who married an Irish princess, but renounced his throne and became a hermit after losing his wife and child to a pack of wolves. His fourteenth-century shrine survives in the neighbouring church. St Morwenna's well at Morwenstow in Cornwall, appears halfway down the cliff-face; it was restored by the eccentric Victorian poet-priest Stephen Hawker. The holy well near Crom Castle, Co. Fermanagh, was once famous for its healing powers.

The Tomb as Sacred Place

The Oriental Museum at Kedleston Hall exhibits a fragment of the cover of the Ka'aba, the *Kiswa*. A new elaborately-embroidered *Kiswa* is provided every year, and the old one cut up for gift or sale to pilgrims. Curzon probably acquired this in 1883 in Cairo, where such pieces were used as charms.

Making the City Sacred

Another guildhall owned by the National Trust is that of the Guild of St George in King's Lynn, Norfolk, built around 1420.

Questioning the Sacred Place

Two other baptism places are the baptism pool at Cwmdu, Carmarthen, and Monksthorpe Baptist Chapel, Lincolnshire, which was converted from a barn in 1701 and is one of only two chapels in the country to retain an outdoor baptismal tank.

A Place to Remember

Memorialising war is linked to both place and time. A ceremony of remembrance takes place around the 11th/12th May each year at the Parachute Regiment memorial at Hardwick Hall, Derbyshire, where the regiment was formed in 1941. The cross that originally marked the grave of Thomas Riversdale Colyer-Fergusson is now in the chapel of his family home of Ightham Mote in Kent. He died in the action that won him the VC on 31st July 1917 at Bellewaarde, Belgium.

Holy Land and 'Crusade'

The idea of 'holy war' is deeply embedded in many cultures. At Powis Castle there is a painted Sicilian peasant cart with illustrations of Roger of Sicily returning from crusade.

The Holy Mountain

Another St Michael's Mount, also known as The Holy Mountain, is Ysgyrid Fawr, a prominent hill outside Abergavenny, Monmouthshire. At the top are traces of St Michael's Chapel, which seems to have been a pilgrimage centre long after the Reformation. In 1680 a Mr Arnold testified that: 'He hath seen a hundred papists meet on the top of an high Hill, called St Michael's Mount, here is frequent meetings eight or ten times in the year, as he is informed. Mass is said, and sometimes Sermons are preached there'. Another witness said that: 'He saw very great numbers of people at their Devotion on the top of a high hill in Monmouthshire called St Michael's Mount, where there is a ruinous Chappel and a stone with crosses on it, which he took to be an Alter and that he hath seen people with Beads in their Hands kneeling towards the said stone, both within and without the Chappel and he has been informed that Mass is often said there.'

Within living memory, local farmers would spread 'holy soil' from the hill on the floors of their byres in the belief that their sick cattle would be cured.

Festivals in the Landscape

May Hill in Gloucestershire is the scene of dancing, and formerly a mock battle, on May Day.

FURTHER READING

The following are just a few references which may prove useful in following up particular themes or sites.

In addition, the National Trust publishes guidebooks to all its larger properties.

General

CARMICHAEL, David L., *Sacred Sites, Sacred Places; One World Archaeology 23*, Routledge (1997) (*See especially* the Introduction)
ELIADE, Mircea, *Patterns in Comparative Religion*, Sheed & Ward (1958) (*See especially* Chapter 10: 'Sacred Places')
HOLM, Jean (ed.), *Sacred Place*, Pinter (1994)
PARK, Chris, *Sacred Worlds: an Introduction to Geography and Religion*, Routledge (1994) (*See* Chapter 8: 'Sacred places and Pilgrimage')

Avebury: Prehistoric Ceremonial Landscape

MALONE, C., *Avebury*, English Heritage (1989)
PITTS, Michael, *Hengeworld*, Arrow (2001)
POLLARD, J. and REYNOLDS, A., *Avebury: the Biography of a Landscape*, Tempus (2002)

Borrowdale: The Sacred Yew

BEVAN-JONES, Robert, *The Ancient Yew: a History of Taxus baccata*, Windgather Press (2002)

Chedworth Roman Villa: Nature Worship

GOODBURN, Roger, *Chedworth Roman Villa*, National Trust Publications (1979)
WALTERS, Bryn, 'Chedworth: Roman Villa or Sanctuary?', *Bulletin of the Association of Roman Archaeology*, No. 9 (Summer 2000)

Clandon Park: Maori Religion and Place

GALLOP, Alan, *The House with the Golden Eyes*, Running Horse Books (1998)
HOOPER-GREENHILL, Eilean, 'Speaking for Herself? Hinemihi and her Discourses', in *Museums and the Interpretation of Visual Culture*, Routledge (2002)
WALKER, Rangini, 'Marae: a Place to Stand', in KING, Michael (ed.), *Te Ao Huhhuri: Aspects of Maoritanga*, Reed Publishing (1992)

Farne Islands: Nature and Celtic Spirituality

BATTISCOMBE, C.F. (ed.), *The Relics of Saint Cuthbert*, Oxford University Press (1956)
WADDELL, Helen (trans.), *Beasts and Saints*, Constable (1934)

Giant's Causeway: Myth and the Landscape

MAIER, Bernhard (trans. Cyril Edwards), *Dictionary of Celtic Religion and Culture*, Boydell (1998)
O'HOGAIN, Daithi (ed.), *Encyclopaedia of Irish Folklore, Legend and Romance*, Ryan (1990)

Glastonbury Tor: New Age and Earth Mysteries

BOWMAN, Marion, 'Drawn to Glastonbury', in Ian READER and Tony WALTER (eds.), *Pilgrimage in Popular Culture*, Macmillan (1993)
BOWMAN, Marion, 'More of the Same? Christianity, Vernacular Religion and Alternative Spirituality in Glastonbury', in Steven SUTCLIFFE and Marion BOWMAN, *Beyond New Age: Exploring Alternative Spirituality*, Edinburgh University Press (2000)
HESELTON, Philip, *Earth Mysteries*, Element (1995)

Greys Court: The Winding Path

SAWARD, Jeff, *Labyrinths and Mazes: the Definitive Guide to Ancient and Modern Traditions*, Gaia Books (2003)
SAWARD, Jeff, *Magical Paths: Labyrinths and Mazes in the 21st Century*, Mitchell Beazley (2002)

Hailes Abbey: Pilgrimage

COLEMAN, Simon and ELSNER, John, *Pilgrimage Past and Present: Sacred Travel and Sacred Space in the World Religions*, British Museum Press (1995)

Holystone: Holy Wells

BORD, Janet and Colin, *Sacred Waters: Holy Wells and Water Lore in Britain and Ireland*, Paladin (1985)
CARROLL, Michael P., *Irish Pilgrimage: Holy Wells and Popular Catholic Devotion*, Johns Hopkins University Press (1999)
HARTE, Jeremy, 'Holy Wells and Other Holy Places', *Living Spring Journal: the International Electronic Forum for Research into Holy Wells & Waterlore* (1 May

2000), available at:
http://www.bath.ac.uk/lispring/journal/issue1/
research/jharhpl1.htm

JONES, Francis, *The Holy Wells of Wales*,
University of Wales Press (1954)

RATTUE, James, *The Living Stream: Holy Wells in
Historical Context*, Boydell (1995)

Housesteads Fort: Mithras and the Cave

CROW, James, *English Heritage Book of
Housesteads*, Batsford/English Heritage (1995)

CUMONT, Franz, *The Mysteries of Mithra*, Dover
Publications (1956) [transl. of French edition, 1896]

DANIELS, C.M., *Mithras Saecularis, the
Housesteads Mithraeum and a Fragment from
Carrawburgh*, Archaeologia Aeliana 40 105–133

VERMASEREN, M.J., Mithras, *The Secret God*, Chatto &
Windus (1963) [transl. of Dutch edition, 1959]

Kedleston Hall: The Tomb as Sacred Place

DICKIE, James, 'Allah and Eternity: Mosques,
Medrasas and Tombs', in MICHELL, George (ed.),
*Architecture of the Islamic World: its History and Social
Meaning*, Thames and Hudson (1978)

The Lake District: The Spiritual Landscape

HILTON, Tim, *John Ruskin* (two vols), Yale University
Press (2000)

NICHOLSON, Norman, *The Lakers: the Adventures
of the First Tourists*, Robert Hale (1955)

RAWNSLEY, E.F., *Canon Rawnsley: an Account of
his Life*, MacLehose, Jackson (1923)

Lavenham Guildhall: Making the City Sacred

BETTERTON, Alec, 'The Guildhall, Lavenham',
History Today 45 (Issue 1, Jan 1995)

RUBIN, Miri, *Corpus Christi: the Eucharist in Late
Medieval Culture*, Cambridge University Press (1991)

Loughwood Meeting House: Questioning the Sacred Place

ARBLASTER, Kate, *Walking Through Time: A Study
of Cwmdu 1850–1920*, Llandeilo: Kate Arblaster,
(2001)

DAVIES, Horton, *Worship and Theology in England
from Watts and Wesley to Maurice, 1690–1850*,
Princeton University Press (1961)

DOWSE, John, *The History of Monksthorpe and
Burgh Baptist Church*, East Midland Baptist Association
(2nd ed. 1994)

WHITELEY, John, *From Backwoods to Beacon:
Kilmington Baptist Church, the First 350 Years* (2000)

Mount Grace Priory: Carthusian Spirituality

BRUCE LOCKHART, Robin, *Halfway to Heaven: The
Hidden Life of the Carthusians*, Darton Longman &
Todd (1999)

KNOWLES, David and HADCOCK, R. Neville,
Medieval Religious Houses: England and Wales,
Longman (1971)

THOMPSON, E. Margaret, *The Carthusian Order in
England*, SPCK (1930)

Mow Cop: Revivalism and Camp Meetings

WILKES, Arthur and LOVATT, Joseph, *Mow Cop and
the Camp Meeting Movement: Sketches of Primitive
Methodism*, Orphans' Printing Press (1942)

Rosedene, Great Dodford: Keeping religion out...'less parsons and more pigs'

FAULKNER, H.U., *Chartism and the Churches: a
Study in Democracy*, Frank Cass (1970)

HADFIELD, Alice Mary, *The Chartist Land Company*,
David & Charles (1970)

POOLE, Diana, *The Last Chartist Land Settlement*,
The Dodford Society (1999)

ROBSON, Shona, 'Land for the Landless, and Votes
for the Disenfranchised: The History and Archaeology
of Rosedene, a Surviving Chartist Cottage at Dodford
with Grafton, Worcestershire', *The National Trust
Annual Archaeological Review*. No. 8 (1999–2000)

St John's Jerusalem: Holy Land and 'Crusade'

ARMSTRONG, Karen, *A History of Jerusalem: One
City, Three Faiths*, HarperCollins (1996)

BARBER, M. (ed.), *The Military Orders: Fighting for
the Faith and Caring for the Sick*, Variorum (1994)

LARKING, L.B., *The Knights Hospitallers in England*,
Camden Society (1857)

NICHOLSON, H. (ed.), *The Military Orders:*

Welfare and Warfare, Ashgate (1998)

St Mary's, Studley Royal: Gothic Revival

BROOKS, Chris, *The Gothic Revival*, Phaidon (1999)

BROOKS, Chris and SAINT, Andrew, *The Victorian Church: Architecture and Society*, Manchester University Press (1995)

CLARK, Kenneth, *The Gothic Revival: An Essay in the History of Taste* (3rd edn.), John Murray (1962)

St Michael's Mount: The Holy Mountain

ECK, Diana L., 'Mountains', in ELIADE, Mircea (ed.), *The Encyclopedia of Religion*, Vol. 12, Macmillan (1987)

Sandham Memorial Chapel: A Place to Remember

CARLINE, Richard, *Stanley Spencer at War*, Faber & Faber (1978)

ROBINSON, Duncan, *Stanley Spencer*, Phaidon (1990)

Sharow Cross: Sanctuary

COX, J. Charles, *The Sanctuaries and Sanctuary Seekers of Mediaeval England*, G. Allen & Sons (1911)

HALLETT, Cecil, *The Cathedral Church of Ripon: a Short History of the Church and a Description of its Fabric*, Bell's Cathedral Series, George Bell (1901)

WESTERMARCK, Edward, A., *Asylum*, in HASTINGS, James (ed.), *Encyclopædia of Religion and Ethics*, Vol. 2, Clark (1909)

Staunton Harold: Restoring the Altar

DAVIES, Horton, *Worship and Theology in England from Andrewes to Baxter and Fox, 1603–1690*, Princeton University Press (1975)

Sutton Hoo: Place, Power and Paganism

BEDE (transl. Leo Sherley-Price), *A History of the English Church and People*, Penguin Books (1955)

CARVER, Martin, *Sutton Hoo: Burial Ground of Kings?* British Museum Press (1998)

Sutton House: Ghosts and Place

EVANS, Hilary, *Seeing Ghosts: Experiences of the Paranormal*, John Murray (2003)

EVANS, Hilary and HUYGHE, Patrick, *The Field Guide to Ghosts and other Apparitions*, Quill (2000)

SPENCER, John and Anne, *The Encyclopedia of Ghosts and Spirits*, Headline (1992)

Tatton Park: Japanese Gardens

KEANE, Marc, *Japanese Garden Design*, Charles E. Tuttle (1996)

Tŷ Mawr Wybrnant: The Welsh Bible and 'The Land of Saints'

EDWARDS, Richard Tudor, *William Morgan*, John Jones (1968)

LLYWELYN, Dorian, *Sacred Place Chosen People: Land and National Identity in Welsh Spirituality*, University of Wales Press (1999)

Uffington White Horse: Festivals in the Landscape

BERGAMAR, Kate, *Discovering Hill Figures*, Shire Publications (1968)

BUSHAWAY, Bob, *By Rite: Custom, Ceremony and Community in England 1700–1880*, Junction Books (1982)

DARVILL, Timothy *et. al.* (eds), *The Cerne Giant: an Antiquity on Trial*, Oxbow Books (1999)

JUDGE, Roy, *May Day in England: an Introductory Bibliography* (3rd edn.), Folklore Society & Vaughan Williams Memorial Library (1999)

LOCK, G., GOSDEN, C., MILES, D., PALMER, S. and CROMARTY, A., *Uffington White Horse and its Landscape: Investigations at White Horse Hill, Uffington, 1989–95, and Tower Hill, Ashbury, 1993–4*, Thames Valley Landscapes Monograph 18, Oxford Archaeology (2003)

MARCH, H. Colley, *The Giant and the Maypole of Cerne*, Proceedings of the Dorset Natural History and Antiquarian Field Club XXII (1901)

INDEX

ACKNOWLEDGEMENTS

First of all, my grateful thanks to Barbara Mercer, who thought it might work and did so much to make it do so; to Margaret Willes, who said yes and made lots of helpful suggestions; to numerous National Trust staff who drew attention to sites and answered obscure questions quickly and efficiently; to Ani and Peter, who encouraged, supported and put up with it; to Hilary Turner who tried to improve my English; to John Rhodes who understands the Lakes and much else; to the wonderful St Deiniol's Library, Hawarden, and also the libraries of the Society of Antiquaries, University College Chichester and Winchester School of Art; to John Anderson, Diana Poole, Jeff Seward; above all to all those researchers and authors of books, articles, guidebooks and websites, on which this small book entirely depends.

PICTURE CREDITS